Yuqing Xing provides a fascinating, accessible, and timely account of the crucial role of global value chains in powering China's transformation into the world's leading exporter. The book is a "must have" for anybody seeking to understand micro dimensions of the contemporary and future global economy, including the forces pushing China towards an inward-looking strategy in high technology, and the risks thereof.

Etel L. Solingen, *Distinguished Professor, Thomas T. and Elizabeth C. Tierney Chair in Peace and Conflict Studies, University of California, Irvine*

China's rise to become the world's largest exporter is a fascinating topic for academic research. Professor Xing studies it from the perspective of global value chains. The book reveals the secrets of China's fast upgrading in global value chains. China's experience can offer useful lessons to other developing countries.

Yang Yao, *Cheung-Kong Scholar and Liberal Arts Chair Professor Dean, National School of Development, Peking University*

This insightful book by a leading economist of China's international trade and industrial development offers a fascinating analysis that challenges conventional trade theories and input–output models. Focusing on value-added trade and firm-level value chain activities, Xing's decoding of China's economic miracle in the interconnected worlds of global production networks is both compelling and crystal-clear. A must-read for anyone interested in China's recent development and the devastating impact of the Covid-19 pandemic.

Henry Wai-chung Yeung, *Distinguished Professor and Co-Director, Global Production Networks Centre, National University of Singapore*

DECODING
CHINA'S
EXPORT
MIRACLE
A Global Value
Chain Analysis

DECODING
CHINA'S
EXPORT
MIRACLE
A Global Value
Chain Analysis

Yuqing Xing
National Graduate Institute for Policy Studies, Japan

World Scientific

NEW JERSEY · LONDON · SINGAPORE · BEIJING · SHANGHAI · HONG KONG · TAIPEI · CHENNAI · TOKYO

Published by

World Scientific Publishing Co. Pte. Ltd.

5 Toh Tuck Link, Singapore 596224

USA office: 27 Warren Street, Suite 401-402, Hackensack, NJ 07601

UK office: 57 Shelton Street, Covent Garden, London WC2H 9HE

Library of Congress Cataloging-in-Publication Data
Names: Xing, Yuqing, author.
Title: Decoding China's export miracle : a global value chain analysis /
    Yuqing Xing, National Graduate Institute for Policy Studies, Japan.
Description: New Jersey : World Scientific, [2021] |
    Includes bibliographical references and index.
Identifiers: LCCN 2020051962 | ISBN 9789811229626 (hardcover) | ISBN
    9789811229633 (ebook) | ISBN 9789811229640 (ebook other)
Subjects: LCSH: Exports--China. | China--Commerce. | China--Economic policy. |
    China--Foreign economic relations.
Classification: LCC HF1416.6.C6 X56 2021 | DDC 382/.60951--dc23
LC record available at https://lccn.loc.gov/2020051962

British Library Cataloguing-in-Publication Data
A catalogue record for this book is available from the British Library.

For any available supplementary material, please visit
https://www.worldscientific.com/worldscibooks/10.1142/12080#t=suppl

Desk Editors: Balasubramanian Shanmugam/Lixi Dong

Typeset by Stallion Press
Email: enquiries@stallionpress.com

Printed in Singapore

To my parents XING Liuzhi and LI Ruifen

for always loving and supporting me

Preface

In the last three decades, two significant phenomena have had great impact on the world economy. First, China has emerged as the global champion of exports and the No. 1 exporting nation of high-technology products. Second, international trade has morphed into trade in tasks dominated by global value chains (GVCs).

The two phenomena are inextricably intertwined. On the one hand, China's integration with the world economy has offered multinational corporations (MNCs) an excellent opportunity to extend their value chains into China and take advantage of the enormous supply of cheap Chinese labor; on the other hand, GVCs have offered a short-cut for made/assembled in China goods to enter international markets, and Chinese firms' deep involvement in value chains in the global manufacturing industry has dramatically accelerated China's industrialization and the expansion of Chinese exports.

When China surpassed Germany in 2009 to become the largest exporting nation in the world, it was just a middle-income country with per capita GDP less than $4,000; its GDP was less than half that of the US, the largest economy in the world. That achievement was accomplished within three decades of China's voluntarily opening of its doors to the rest of the world in the late 1970s. It's no exaggeration to say that China's emergence as the world No.1

exporter is an unprecedented event in the history of world economic development, bordering on the miraculous.

Many theories have been offered to explain this export miracle, mostly focusing on China's comparative advantage in labor-intensive goods, its institutional reforms, its exchange rate regimes, its internal and external trade liberalization, and the inflows of export-oriented foreign direct investment. This book, however, goes beyond those factors, which mainly emphasize trade barriers and costs of goods. It examines China's export miracle in the context of GVCs, and highlights the importance of the international division of labor between Chinese firms and the MNCs that operate and manage value chains to which Chinese manufacturers belong. Working from its examination of value chains for the production of specific high-technology products and processing exports, this book analyzes the intrinsic linkages between Chinese exports and GVCs, the tasks in which Chinese firms specialize, and the mechanism by which GVCs have powered the rapid growth of Chinese exports. The results of the analysis reveal that the participation of Chinese firms in GVCs, which are led by foreign MNCs, has been a major factor contributing to the tremendous success of made/assembled in China products in the global market. The spillover effects of brands; technology and product innovation; and global distribution and retail networks (which are the contribution of foreign MNCs within the division of labor along value chains) have systematically eliminated conventional entry barriers to international markets for made/assembled in China products, thus greatly facilitating the massive penetration of Chinese goods into the markets of both developed and developing countries — and in essence powering China's export miracle. To a large extent, the worldwide popularity and competitiveness of made/assembled in China products can be attributed to the spillover effects of GVCs.

The proliferation of GVCs has seen trade in goods replaced by trade in tasks, where a number of firms located in various nations jointly deliver ready-to-use products to consumers in the global market. In the age of GVCs, the comparative advantage of an individual country cannot decide the competitiveness of products manufactured and traded along value chains. For some time now China has been a major hub of manufacturing-based value chains. China's trade patterns and the roots of its export miracle are much more visible and clearly defined when viewed through the lens of GVCs.

This is the first book to systematically investigate the Chinese miracle from the perspective of GVCs rather than those of classic comparative advantage theory, institutional reforms and trade liberalization. The GVC approach affords a rational solution to many puzzles surrounding the miracle, such as why at one point China accounted for almost half of the US trade deficit in goods; how China, a developing country, could surpass the US, Japan and the 27 EU countries and turn into the No.1 exporting nation of high-technology goods; and how China has become the largest apparel exporter even though it does not have a single globally recognized fashion brand. Compared with the East Asian miracle of the successful development experiences of Japan and the Four Asian Tigers, Chinese firms' involvement in GVCs is unprecedented in scope and scale, which constitutes a flagship feature of China's development model.

The dominance of GVCs in the manufacture of goods and in international trade has challenged the reliability of conventional trade statistics for the measurement of value chain trade. For instance, current trade statistics cannot trace the international trade activities of factoryless manufacturers, which mainly derive their earnings from intangible assets and services embedded in physical goods made/assembled by foreign contract manufacturers. In the context of China–US trade, this book addresses the distortion by conventional trade statistics of the trade imbalance between the two countries through consideration of two phenomena: the foreign value added embedded in Chinese exports and the value added derived by Apple from its sales in the Chinese market. The former has led to a significant exaggeration of China's exports to and trade surplus with the US, while the latter leads to the underestimation of US exports to China. The book also highlights the deterioration of the impact of currency depreciation on value chain trade, and identifies a new channel through which exchange rates affect GVC-dominated international trade.

GVCs are a micro phenomenon. To give the reader an understanding of the critical role of GVCs in promoting Chinese exports, and of the dependence of the Chinese miracle on GVCs, this book examines Chinese firms' involvement in the value chains of specific products including iPhones and high-technology industry and processing exports, so as to elucidate the international division of labor between Chinese firms and MNCs along value chains. In particular, the book analyzes processing export statistics to measure the dependence of Chinese exports on GVCs. That direct measurement not only avoids the technical complexity of the input-output table approach, but also preserves the fundamental characteristics of value chain organizations. The measurement is a more accurate quantification of the dependence of Chinese exports on GVCs than that using the popular GVC participation indexes defined in the OECD TiVA database.

At present, China is the largest assembler of mobile phones in the world, and three out of the five top global smartphone brands are Chinese. The rise of the Chinese mobile phone industry illustrates the benefits of GVCs for developing nations who have been struggling to tap international markets, in particular the booming markets for information and communications technology. This book traces the path of the Chinese mobile phone industry along the GVC of mobile phones, where China began as a simple assembler for foreign mobile phone vendors, gradually moved to high-value added segments, and eventually developed home-grown brands Huawei, Xiaomi and OPPO, which are competitive with those of Samsung and Apple. Before developing core technology capacity such as operating system design and mobile phone chipset production, those Chinese firms leapt forward to brand development and became lead firms in the mobile phone industry. This non-linear innovation path reflects the flexibility of GVC strategy for catch-up by developing countries.

The last three decades have been the golden age of GVC development. Economic efficiency was the single driver of the spread of GVCs across countries. Unprecedented globalization created a favorable environment where Chinese firms could plug into GVCs and adopt GVC growth strategy, all of which fueled the rapid growth of Chinese exports. However, the ongoing US–China trade war has exposed the vulnerability of China-centered GVCs. As the trade war has evolved into a technology war, Chinese high-technology firms such as Huawei, sanctioned by the US government, have been struggling to stabilize their supply chains, where American technologies have long been indispensable. The possible technology decoupling between China and the US may signal a significant reshuffling of existing GVCs and a return to inward looking development strategy in China, especially in high-technology development. That high-pressure development is compounded by the unfolding COVID-19 pandemic, which has not only disrupted the smooth operations of GVCs, but also thrown into question the wisdom of using GVCs to produce essential drugs and personal protective equipment, when all nations are facing the unexpected health crisis. As more and more sovereign governments embark on the pursuit of self-sufficiency in medical supplies, the contraction of GVCs for the sake of national security may be inevitable. At the end of this book, I discuss possible trajectories of China-centered GVCs in the aftermath of the US–China trade war and the COVID-19 pandemic.

=◇=

The first draft of this book, completed when I was visiting the East Asian Institute (EAI) of the National University of Singapore (NUS) on a sabbatical leave from May 2019 to June 2020, brought together the results of my long-term research on GVCs, a journey on which I set out a decade earlier. After the Singapore government implemented the circuit breaker to contain the spread of the COVID-19 in early April, 2020, I had basically locked myself down at my NUS apartment until my return to Tokyo in late June. Ironically, the lockdown forced me to concentrate on writing the book and improved my productivity. The worldwide domino effects triggered by the Chinese lockdown reinforced my belief that GVCs have been a catalyst of China's export growth.

I am grateful to the National Graduate Institute for Policy Studies for granting me the privilege of the sabbatical leave, which enabled me to concentrate on the book project and complete it successfully. During my stay at EAI, I benefited greatly from discussions with my colleagues there, most of them Chinese studies scholars. In particular, I would like to thank Professor Bert Hofman, the director of EAI and former World Bank Country Director for China, for his generous support of this book project.

Mr. John West, my former colleague at Asian Development Bank Institute and long-term friend, is the first reader of the draft manuscript. I am indebted for his insightful comments, which prompted me to add one chapter on the trajectory of GVCs under the twin shadows of the US–China trade war and the COVID-19 pandemic.

Last but not least, I would like to thank Mr. Lawrie Hunter, editor at the Center for Professional Communication at the National Graduate Institute for Policy Studies. His professional editing has significantly improved the readability of the manuscript.

About the Author

 **Dr. Yuqing Xing** is a Professor of Economics at the National Graduate Institute for Policy Studies (GRIPS) in Tokyo. He served as the Director of the Capacity Building and Training Department of the Asian Development Bank Institute from 2011 to 2014. He also held positions at World Institute for Development Economics Research, the Bank of Finland, and the East Asian Institute of the National University of Singapore. He has provided consulting services to Asian Development Bank, International Monetary Fund, and Japan International Cooperation Agency.

Dr. Xing's research focuses on global value chains, international trade, foreign direct investment, exchange rates, and Chinese economy. He is a leading expert on global value chains. His research on the iPhone and the China–US trade balance has been discussed widely in the global mainstream media, challenging conventional views on bilateral trade statistics, and instigating a reform of trade statistics.

Dr. Xing received his Bachelor's and Master's degrees from Peking University, China, and his PhD in Economics from the University of Illinois at Urbana–Champaign, USA.

Contents

List of Figures

List of Tables

Chapter 1

Introduction

Today, "Made in China" products are ubiquitous in markets in both developed and developing countries. It is no exaggeration to say that we can surely find Chinese goods in any shop anywhere in the world. In Tokyo, New York, Sydney, Paris, any place you can think of, Chinese products are indispensable for the daily life of the local residents. If some patriotic consumers tried to avoid Chinese products, their daily life would be rather painful. In her book, *A Year Without "Made in China": One Family's True Life Adventure in the Global Economy*, American journalist Sara Bongiorni (2008) recorded the difficulties her family encountered after she initiated a one-year experiment, living without made in China products. During that year, her family used considerable time searching for, and spent disproportionate money on, non-Chinese goods. Her kids had no candles for their birthday parties, they could not play any games, and they spent a Christmas without traditional decorations — because they could not find any of those goods that were not made in China. After the painful one-year experience, Mrs. Bongiorni concluded that, these days there is not a chance for life without China.

Four decades ago, China was a centrally planned economy, virtually isolated from the rest of the world. "Independence and self-reliance" was not just a political slogan; it was an essential principle guiding Chinese government officials in the formulation of economic plans. The reforms and open-door policy introduced in 1978 marked a paradigm shift in the course of Chinese economic development. Now, after four decades of rapid growth, China has emerged as the world's leading exporting nation, with more than $2 trillion yearly in exports of goods and services, a remarkable achievement. Even Deng Xiaoping, the chief architect of the open-door policy, could not have imagined that in less than 30 years, China would surpass Japan, US and Germany to emerge as the largest exporting country and the global center of manufacturing, supplying the whole world with a wide variety of products, ranging from labor-intensive products such as shoes, T-shirts and sweaters, to high-technology products including smartphones, laptop computers and drones.

According to Angus Maddison (2001), a renowned scholar of economic growth history, in 1500 A.D. ancient China was the largest, most prosperous economy in the world, accounting for about a quarter of world gross domestic product (GDP). Under its autarky, ancient China had achieved the economic prosperity. International trade was irrelevant. Now, in the 21st century, China has returned to its economic glory of the 16th century and grew into a $14 trillion economy, the second largest in the world, just behind the US. That tremendous success, however, was accomplished only after China voluntarily integrated itself with the rest of the world and embraced an export-led growth strategy. It achieved this economic prosperity as an open economy.

Exports have been one of the most important growth engines of the Chinese economy. The explosive growth of exports in the last four decades played a central role in the sustained economic growth of China. Development economists and China watchers have attempted to explain the dramatic growth of China's exports, and have sought to identify the critical factors enabling the extensive and successful penetration of Chinese exports in the global market. A plethora of such studies and articles have been published in academic journals, magazines and newspapers. The factors identified as major contributors to China's export miracle include China's comparative advantage in labor-intensive goods; the Chinese government's policy of promoting exports; the pegging of the Chinese yuan to the dollar exchange rate regime; inflows of export-oriented foreign direct investment (FDI); China's entry into the World Trade Organization (WTO); and the advance of worldwide trade liberalization. There is no disputing that these factors helped transform China from a closed to an open economy, substantially enhanced the growth of Chinese exports and facilitated the penetration of made in China products into international markets. Nonetheless, those factors are far from sufficient to explain why China, a developing country, could emerge as the leading exporter of high-technology products, and why almost half of the US trade deficit originated in China, whose GDP was less than 15 percent of global GDP, and why made in China products are more competitive than goods from both developing countries and developed countries.

As a matter of fact, most made in China products available in international markets are sold under foreign brands. Until now, even in the category of labor-intensive products such as shoes, toys and apparel, where Chinese firms are thought to have comparative advantage, there are no Chinese brands which are internationally recognized and able to compete with foreign brands such as Nike, ZARA and UNIQLO. A revealing question: without foreign brands, could China export the volume of goods that it does today? Despite the rapid economic growth of the last four decades, China is still at the catching-up stage, having just achieved middle-income country status. In 2019, China's GDP per capita passed the $10,000 mark, which is still less than one-fifth of that of the US. Less than 20 percent of the Chinese labor force has a college education. There are few industries where Chinese indigenous firms are world leaders. How could China have a trade surplus of more than $130 billion with the US in high-technology products, an area where the US is seen as having a comparative advantage? Such questions cannot be answered by conventional trade theory, with its emphasis on comparative advantage in labor productivity or resource endowments. To gain a clear understanding of China's export miracle, we have to turn away from classic comparative advantage theory and exchange rate regime and trade liberalization arguments, and examine the organization of the production underlying Chinese exports, the channels by which Chinese exports enter international markets, and the country origins of core technologies embedded in Chinese exports.

Close examination of the production of Chinese exports, in particular exports to the US, reveals that Chinese exports are mainly manufactured and traded along global value chains (GVCs), which in the last few decades have brought about fundamental changes in trade patterns, in the comparative advantage of each nation, and in the organization of international trade. As mentioned by Grossman and Rossi-Hansberg (2008), today's trade has moved on: it differs significantly from the cloth for wine trade discussed by the British economist David Ricardo some 200 years ago. Modern international trade has evolved from trade in goods to trade in tasks. Almost all manufacturing products are now produced and traded along GVCs, in which many firms located in geographically dispersed countries are involved in tasks ranging from research and development to the final delivery of products to end users in global markets. Technological innovations and extensive outsourcing by multinational corporations (MNCs) now direct and amplify trade flows, reshaping geographic trade patterns and balances.

The emergence of GVCs has revolutionized the nature and scope of export-oriented economic growth. The international division of labor in the world economy has evolved from the level of goods and industries to the more granular level of tasks, "the second unbundling," to use a term coined by Professor Richard Baldwin (2018). The fragmentation of production on a global scale provides numerous opportunities for Chinese firms to participate in value chains and take advantage of spillover effects from GVCs. To a large extent, the successful penetration of Chinese exports into international markets has been driven by GVCs, where Chinese firms perform production tasks such as assembly, while lead firms of GVCs are responsible for research and development, product design, brand promotion and marketing. In general, firms selling products in foreign markets face a variety of fixed costs, such as distribution channel setup; acquisition of an understanding of foreign regulations and consumer preferences; production of commercials for product promotion. Those fixed costs are usually an obstacle to firms in their efforts to export their products to international markets (Melitz, 2003). Chinese firms circumvent those obstacles by participating in GVCs governed by foreign MNCs with internationally recognized brands, advanced technology, and global distribution and retail networks. GVCs have actually functioned as a special channel for made in China products to enter the global market.

Three GVC spillover effects that benefited Chinese firms involved in value chains managed by MNCs have been a decisive factor of China's emergence as the world's No.1 exporting nation and the champion of high-technology exports. One spillover effect comes from the brands owned by lead firms of GVCs. By plugging into value chains as contract manufacturers, Chinese firms have sold their products under internationally recognized brands, the labels of which clearly have enhanced the appeal of those made in China products to foreign consumers and strengthened their competitiveness. The second spillover effect is the technology and product innovation of GVC lead firms, which constantly nurtures new markets and develops demand for new products. The production of any high-technology products requires both high value-added components and low value-added parts and services. By participating in GVCs, for example, the value chain of the iPhone, and specializing in low value added tasks (e.g., assembly), Chinese firms have been able to join the value creation processes of high-technology products and benefited from the fast growing worldwide demand for those products. The third spillover effect of GVCs is related to the distribution and retail networks established by GVC lead firms. As suppliers of foreign MNCs, Chinese firms have gained easy access to international markets, and their products have been sold through retail stores operated by GVC lead firms. In addition to the benefit of low costs, often emphasized in mainstream discussions, the three spillover effects are crucial determinants of China's export miracle.

Not only did GVCs open a door for Chinese firms to access international markets, they also offered an alternative path by which China could achieve industrialization. Offshoring by GVC lead firms brings countries like China production capabilities that would take them decades to develop domestically. More importantly, plugging into a GVC is akin to engaging in a dynamic learning curve. The learning opportunities associated with GVC participation have significantly enhanced the innovation in and upgrading of processing by Chinese firms involved in value chains. Low value-added tasks such as assembling mobile phones, sewing jeans and stitching shoes were entry points for Chinese firms to take part in value chains. There is a widely voiced concern that firms from developing countries may be trapped in low value-added segments of GVCs, either because they do not have the requisite learning capacity or because lead firms deliberately withhold their production know-how and technology from non-lead firms (Sturgeon and Kawakami, 2010). The impressive upgrading of Chinese firms in various industries demonstrates that the "low value-added trap" does not exist in China. Furthermore, Chinese firms have learned how to use value chain strategy to achieve nonlinear upgrading — bypassing the requisite technological stages and jumping directly to brand development. Now, of the top five global smartphone brands, three are Chinese: Huawei, OPPO and Xiaomi. All three emerged by sourcing core technologies, such as operating systems, central processing units (CPUs) and memory chips, from foreign countries. Those Chinese companies are now GVC lead firms, despite their technology shortcomings.

The rise of GVCs in international trade challenges the way in which economists assess national comparative advantage. For quite some time economists have used revealed comparative advantage as a proxy for national comparative advantage. To date, value chain trade is the dominant form of exports and imports, and as a result conventional trade statistics are not suitable for assessing comparative advantage and dynamic change in trade structures. Revealed comparative advantage, computed with gross values of trade, tends to overstate China's comparative advantage in the sectors where imports constitute a significant portion of intermediate inputs, especially in high-technology sectors where finished products are used as a measure of the technology content of exports (Ma *et al.*, 2015). According to UNCOMTRADE database, in 2018 China accounted for about 70 percent of the world exports of laptop computers and handheld tablets. Applying the formula for revealed comparative advantage, we might hastily conclude that China has a revealed comparative advantage in the production of laptop computers and handheld tablets. However, the core technologies of laptop computers, operating systems and CPUs are monopolized by American companies Microsoft, Apple, Intel and AMD. The conclusion that China has comparative advantage in those products is unfounded. These contradictory conclusions regarding phenomena such as China's export of iPhones to the US and China's world leadership in high-technology exports, reflect an improper interpretation of trade statistics that fails to identify sources of core technologies and cannot distinguish between skilled tasks and assembly. Those interpretations mistakenly suggest, for example, that everything shipped out of China was made there and represented technology advancement there. Chinese firms' participation in GVCs enables them to perform low-skilled tasks in the context of the manufacture of high-technology products. This does not necessarily mean that those firms have acquired the skills, technology and production know-how required for the independent creation of high-technology products.

GVCs involve complicated trade relations between nations. Apparently bilateral trade relations are in fact multilateral. The triangular trade formed by production networks in Asia is a case in point. At the center of the triangular trade, China imports intermediate inputs from Japan, Taiwan, Korea, Singapore and other Asian economies, assembles them into finished products, and eventually exports them to the US (Wang, 1995). The gross value of China's exports includes not only domestic value added but also the value added of other Asian economies. As a result, the Chinese goods produced via those production networks and eventually sold in the US market actually reflect exports of both China and the other

Asian countries involved. Following the same logic, some part of the trade imbalance between China and the US is multilateral rather than bilateral, and a substantial part of China's trade surplus with the US consists of transfers from other Asian economies via the production networks.

However, the current system of trade statistics assessment is designed for the classic cloth for wine trade; it is not suitable for analysis of value chain based modern trade. Despite the dominance of GVCs in international trade, economists, policy makers and politicians still rely on conventional trade statistics methodology for their analyses of trade patterns, bilateral trade balances, trade structures, and national comparative advantage. The economic implications of current trade statistics are misleading for examination of the above economic concepts in the context of value chain trade. For example, the inconsistency between value chain based modern trade and conventional trade statistics technique seriously distorts the bilateral trade balance between China and the US. Conventional trade statistics measure the gross value of goods when they cross national borders, implicitly assuming that the entire gross value is produced domestically by the exporting country. That assumption has long been a fundamental element of trade debates, negotiations and the evaluation of the export capacity of nations — but it is not valid for value chain trade. The value added of a product manufactured along a value chain cannot be attributed to any single country. Rather, it is distributed among the countries that take part in the manufacturing process. The gross value of Chinese exports to the US is an aggregate of Chinese domestic value added and various foreign value added. China has for some time been the center of global manufacturing assembly, and most of its exports to the US are composed of imported intermediate inputs, so conventional trade statistics, which aggregate domestic and foreign value added, unquestionably exaggerate China's export volume and its trade surplus with the US, and thus generate misleading information about China's trade structure as well as the markup on its technology.

On the other hand, now in the age of GVCs, conventional trade statistics actually understate US exports to China. The new international division of labor along GVCs has transformed many American MNCs into factoryless centers of product design and technology innovation. When factoryless American MNCs employ contract manufacturers located outside the US to produce or assemble their products (e.g., Qualcomm chips, GAP clothes, and iPhones) and then sell those products to Chinese consumers, those "American goods" are not counted as a US export to China, because they are not exported from the US. The brands, technologies and services to which factoryless American MNCs contribute and own the intellectual property rights to, generally account for a very large share of the value added of their products sold in the Chinese market. When Chinese consumers purchase these products, they pay not only for the production costs but also for the value added associated with intellectual property and services embedded in the products. However, current trade statistics practice is not capable of tracing transactions in this new type of trade, or of recording the value added of American factoryless manufacturers, such as the value added of their intangible assets derived from the Chinese market. Hence, a substantial portion of exports to China by American factoryless manufacturers is "missing" in the statistics recording bilateral trade flows between the two nations. Using current trade statistics to examine the bilateral trade not only inflates China's export volume but also underestimates the volume of US exports, resulting in considerable distortion of the trade balance — which has been the focus of trade frictions between the two nations.

The prevalence of GVCs also challenges the conventional wisdom regarding the relations between exchange rates and trade. Chinese exports generally consist of both domestic and foreign value added. Regardless of whether Chinese firms have pricing power and thus can engage in exchange rate pass-through, the appreciation of the yuan can only affect the portion of value added generated in China, not all the value added of Chinese exports, as assumed by the classic theory. In the case of China–US trade, most Chinese exports to the US are in the form of processing exports; the pass-through effect of yuan appreciation, if such exists, is sharply discounted by the presence of foreign value added. Additionally, along value chains, Chinese firms are in charge of production, while foreign MNCs take care of global distribution and retailing. The value added by Chinese firms is relatively small compared to the retail prices paid by consumers for made in China products. A small increase in production costs due to the appreciation of the yuan may not necessarily translate as an increase in final prices. In open macroeconomics models, imports proxy domestic demand for foreign goods and services. Countries participating in GVCs need to import a large amount of parts and components to produce exports. The quantity of imports used as inputs of those exports (processing imports in the case of China) is actually determined by foreign demand, not domestic demand. Therefore, imports used for the production of exports do not respond in the conventional fashion to the movements of yuan exchange rates.

GVCs have brought revolutionary changes to international trade and challenges to the standard economic theories that have shaped the mindsets of both economists and policy makers in their analysis of and debates about international trade and policies. This book adopts the GVC approach to analyze the Chinese export miracle over the last four decades. It is a new approach, different from the Ricardian comparative advantage, the Heckscher–Ohlin model and the new trade theory based on economies of scale as developed by Professor Paul Krugman. It focuses on value added rather than gross value of exports, and on tasks rather than finished products, in its calculation of bilateral trade balances, evaluation of national comparative advantage, and identification of trade patterns and structures of exports. Value added in trade can alleviate distortions caused by current trade statistics methodology, and thus can accurately depict national competitiveness in international markets.

Following the GVC approach, this book extends the coverage of exports from tangibles to intangibles (intellectual property and services embedded in tangible products sold to foreign consumers). A recent phenomenon sees MNCs from developed nations transformed into factoryless manufacturers, primarily deriving their revenues from services and intellectual property embedded in tangible products assembled by foreign contract manufacturers, while firms from developing countries specialize in manufacturing and assembly. The US and China represent the extremes of the trend. Counting the value added of factoryless manufacturers as part of their home-country exports will enable an accurate understanding of how developed countries benefit from globalization in the age of GVCs. It will also mitigate the bias in trade statistics methods of assessing bilateral trade balances between developed and developing countries, notably that between China and the US.

The GVC approach can systematically explain how in less than four decades China evolved from a closed economy to the world's leading exporting nation, why China — a developing country, exported more high-technology products than labor-intensive products to the US, and why almost half of the US trade deficit originated from China.

Regarding the ongoing US–China trade war, the GVC approach provides a new perspective on the detrimental effects of the punitive tariffs imposed by the Trump administration on Chinese goods and why many foreign MNCs have chosen to relocate part of their supply chains outside of China during the trade war.

The theoretical arguments and empirical evidence presented in this book are mainly drawn from my studies of Chinese exports and GVCs over the last decade. I came up with the idea of analyzing China's export miracle from the perspective of GVCs in 2009, when I was visiting the National University of Singapore's East Asian Institute (EAI), a research institute well-known for its focus on contemporary China Studies. At that time, I was working on a project concerning China's high-technology exports. I was intrigued by a report claiming that in 2007 China ranked No. 1 in high-technology exports and that its annual high-technology exports exceeded those of the US, Japan and the 27 EU countries respectively (Meri, 2009). As a Chinese raised in China, I was thrilled by the statement, "China was the No. 1 high-technology exporting nation." At that time, though, my personal understanding of the technology capacity of Chinese firms and the roles they performed in manufacturing high-technology products for foreign markets had me thinking that the statement was too good to be true. The rapid growth of Chinese high-technology exports, as reported by conventional trade statistics, had attracted the attention of many scholars. In 2006, Professor Dani Rodrik, a famous development economist at Harvard University, published an article entitled, "What is so special about China's exports?" (Rodrik, 2006). Rodrik found that the share of high-technology products in Chinese exports was extraordinarily high, even higher than that of developed nations. He credited the rapid growth of Chinese high-technology exports to the Chinese government's science and technology policy. I have no doubt that China's investment in research and development and its policy governing technological innovation have enhanced the technology capacity of Chinese firms and narrowed the technology gap between China and advanced economies. Given that China remains a developing country in spite of its fast growth over the last 40 years, I do not believe China's accumulated technological capability was sufficient to transform China into the No. 1 high-technology exporting nation. The dependence of Chinese high-technology exports on foreign technologies, in particular the core technologies essential for technological functions, implies that China as a high-technology export champion was a myth rather than a reality.

To what extent do high-technology products assembled by Chinese firms reflect their technological capacity? Is it reasonable to use assembled products such as the iPhone to proxy the technology advancement of Chinese firms? With those questions in mind, I investigated how China's high-technology products were produced, and examined the ownership structure of the Chinese firms exporting high-technology goods. The findings were consistent with my intuition that China was still far from being a real high-technology champion. More than 80 percent of Chinese high-technology exports in 2010 were processing exports, made with imported parts and components, most of which were core technology parts. It was the foreign technologies that determined the advanced technological features and functions of Chinese high-technology exports. The dominance of processing exports is evidence that the dramatic increase of Chinese high-technology exports was a result of Chinese firms' integration into GVCs. In my summary of those findings in a paper, "China's high-technology exports: myth and reality," I suggested that this kind of exports should be referred to as "assembled high-technology" rather than "high-technology" (Xing, 2014).

Upon my return from Singapore, I bought my first iPhone, an iPhone 3G with a black cover. I had not been a fan of mobile phones before the arrival of the iPhone. I was so impressed by the touch screen, the virtual keyboard and the seamless integration of mobile phone and music player functions. While I was enjoying the phone, I was struck by a statement printed on the back of the phone: "Designed by Apple in California Assembled in China." I had bought thousands of made in China products, including T-shirts, jeans, computers, TVs, and microwaves in Japan, the US, Canada and other countries I had visited or lived in. Made in China had been a standard label for products exported by China, specifying their country of origin, as required by WTO regulations. That was the first time I saw the phrase, "Assembled in China." I had never seen a similar statement on any other Chinese product available on international markets. I had no clue why Steve Jobs ignored the tradition and used "Assembled in China." The statement unambiguously describes the role of Chinese firms involved in the manufacture of the iPhone. In essence, they follow Apple's design and assemble imported parts and components into ready-to-use iPhones. The iPhone is an intuitively clear example of the growth of Chinese high-technology exports being driven by GVCs rather than by the advancement of China's indigenous technology.

In 2008, the world economy was engulfed in a global financial crisis that dragged the US into the worst economic recession since the Great Depression of the 1930s, wiping out almost $8 trillion in wealth in the US stock market (Merie, 2018). A few European countries, notably Greece, Spain, Ireland and Portugal, stumbled into sovereign debt crises. Macroeconomists from the US Federal Reserve Banks, the International Monetary Fund (IMF), the Central Bank of the European Union and the academic community searched for reasons for the crisis and attempted to draft policy recommendations to prevent the world from falling into another similar crisis. Global imbalances, in which some nations (for example, China) have current account surpluses while others (of which the US is a clear example) have current account deficits, had been singled out as a key factor contributing to that economic turmoil (*The Economist*, 2009; Portes, 2009). At the center of those global imbalances was the imbalance between China and the US: China had the largest current account surplus, while the US had the largest current account deficit. Trade surplus was the major element of China's current account surplus and trade deficit the major element of the US current account deficit. It appears that China's rebalancing was expected to be the key to the rebalancing of the global economy. Significant appreciation of the Chinese yuan was suggested by many economists, including Nobel laureate Paul Krugman (2010), whose article, "Taking on China" in the *New York Times* urged the US government to pressure the Chinese government to revalue the Chinese yuan.

In the age of GVCs, would the appreciation of the yuan be as effective as expected by its proponents? I have my doubts. In the mindset of those macroeconomists, Chinese exports are similar to the exports examined by British economist David Ricardo two centuries ago, but in reality they are not. Before 2007, more than half of Chinese exports were in the form of processing exports, i.e., they were made with imported foreign intermediates and traded along value chains controlled by foreign MNCs. The exchange rate elasticity of Chinese exports would be too small to affect China's exports or its trade balance. To test the aforementioned hypothesis, I analyzed the exchange rate elasticity of China's processing trade. I was surprised to find that processing exports contributed more than 100 percent of China's trade surplus, and the Marshall–Lerner condition, a theoretically sufficient condition for a country's trade balance to fall when its currency appreciates, did not hold for China's processing trade because processing imports would fall as the yuan appreciated. As I cast for an example demonstrating the correctness of my findings, the phrase "Designed by Apple in California Assembled in China" came to my mind. I thought that the iPhone might be a convincing case. My former student Mr. Neal Detert, a research associate at the Asian Development Bank Institute (ADBI), helped me collect the teardown data of the iPhone 3G along with relevant iPhone trade statistics. I analyzed the data and got astonishing results. China contributed only a $6.5 assembly service to each iPhone 3G — about 3.6 percent of the total production cost! But the trade statistics added $179 to China's high-technology exports for each iPhone 3G exported to the US, dramatically inflating China's exports to and trade surplus with the US. We summarized the findings in a paper, *How the iPhone Widens the US Trade Deficit with China*, in which we arrived at three major conclusions. First, conventional trade statistics significantly exaggerated the US trade deficit with China, and value added of exports, rather than gross value of exports, should be used to assess the bilateral trade balance between the US and China in the age of GVCs. Second, foreign value added embedded in the iPhone export substantially weakened the impact of exchange rates on the China–US bilateral trade balance, so that even a yuan appreciation of 50 percent would have little impact on China's iPhone exports to the US. The paper concludes with a provocative observation that profit maximization motivated Apple to have iPhones assembled in China.

In July 2010, I presented the paper at the ADBI. The responses of the seminar audiences were lukewarm — except for my colleague John West, who was fascinated by the results. Economists like to use large samples to do econometric analysis; they generally view case analyses as biased and incapable of representing the distribution of a population. In this case, however, we challenge the reliability of current trade statistics practice for the measurement of bilateral trade balances; and the viability of conventional trade theories in interpretations of trade patterns and exchange rate impacts when goods are produced and traded along GVCs. For such purposes, a representative case should be sufficient. Former ADBI Research Director Dr. Mario Lamberte also praised the coherent and elegant analysis in our paper. He recommended initial publication as an ADBI working paper. Recently, partly because of the dominance of the Internet, working papers have become a popular means of disseminating new ideas, especially unorthodox ideas not favored by the editors of mainstream academic journals.

On December 16, 2010, I gave a lecture at Waseda University's Business School. On my way to the lecture room, I picked up a free copy of the *Wall Street Journal* (Asian Edition). As I was browsing the newspaper, I was electrified to see an article on page 3, *Sum of iPhone Parts: Trade Distortion*, by Andrew Batson. There was a full page article summarizing the major findings of my paper, with a colorful, smartly designed chart at the top of the page providing a visual explanation of the way trade statistics distort the US trade deficit with China.

Then on January 10, 2011, the *Wall Street Journal* published an editorial article entitled, *The $6.50 Trade War*. The figure $6.50 refers to the Chinese value added calculated in the iPhone case analysis. The editorial brandished the findings of the iPhone case to criticize American Senator Charles Schumer's proposal that trade sanctions be imposed on China. Those two *Wall Street Journal* articles disseminated our research findings to the global media and attracted huge public attention, some time before the academic community showed any interest. Later, *Time* printed an article by Michael Schuman, *Is the iPhone Bad for the American Economy?* and Klau Meinhardt, the largest business newspaper of Germany published an article entitled, *The Strange Logic of the Global iPhone Economy*.

Shortly thereafter, I was interviewed by Wendy Kaufman of National Public Radio (NPR). During the interview, she asked me a provocative question: "Who asked you to do that research?" I was surprised by her query. I replied, "I have full academic freedom in research in Japan. If you really want me to point to the origin of that study, I think it is the American professors who taught me when I studied in the US. I learned economic analysis from them." I had no idea when NPR would air the interview — then one day, my Ph.D. supervisor, Professor Charles Kolstad, sent me a radio file and told me to check out who was in the radio program. He had listened to the program on his way home. Later, the *New York Times* showed interest in the research. A *New York Times* reporter emailed me and asked me about the employment impact of moving iPhone assembly back to the US. She had assisted in the writing of the Pulitzer Prize winning *New York Times* article, *How the US Lost iPhone Jobs to China*.

The extensive media coverage of the analysis of the iPhone case eventually caught the attention of academic economists. Professor Richard Baldwin, the chief editor of *VOXEU*, invited me to write a column about the iPhone case analysis — I wrote one, and it was published on April 11, 2011. The WTO and IDE-JETRO (2011) published a joint report, *Trade Patterns and Global Value Chains in East Asia: From Trade in Goods to Trade in Tasks*, the first institutional report where world input–output tables were used to estimate the China–US trade balance in value added. Koen De Backer, Head of Division, Directorate for Science, Technology and Innovation of the OECD, replicated the iPhone analysis for the case of the iPhone 4 (Backer, 2011). He found that China's value added to the iPhone 4 was $6.54, a mere $0.04 difference from the estimate in the analysis of the iPhone 3G. In 2012, OECD and WTO (2012) published a joint note, *Trade in Value-Added: Concepts, Methodologies and Challenges*, which declared an official support of the two international organizations for the measurement of trade in value added. Professor Simon Evenett, a member of the editorial board of *Journal Aussenwirtschaft*, invited me to publish the paper in that journal after it was rejected by two mainstream economic journals, *Journal of Economic Perspectives* and *China Economic Review*. Senior research fellow Satoshi Inomata of the IDE-JETRO commented that the iPhone paper was the first to address the "alarming question about the validity of conventional trade statistics based on gross values" (Inomata, 2017). Now, the use of value added in analyses of trade issues is an emerging trend in economic research.

Many scholars and practitioners contacted me and asked if I had updated the analysis on new iPhone models. They were interested in the upgrading of Chinese firms' participation in the iPhone value chain. With the technical assistance of a mobile phone design house in Shenzhen, China, I replicated the teardown analysis for the iPhone X, launched by Apple in 2018. The analysis showed that Chinese firms captured more value added in the new model and performed more sophisticated tasks, well beyond simple assembly. Thanks to Professor Richard Baldwin, the summary of my iPhone X analysis was published promptly in *VOXEU*, appearing on November 11, 2019. It has attracted great interest from both scholars and policy makers. It is evident that the economies of China and the US have been closely integrated by a new invisible hand — GVCs — so the decoupling narrative is almost impossible.

Now many paradoxes regarding China's export miracle can be resolved from the GVC perspective. The unprecedented rapid growth of the Chinese economy in the last four decades has prompted debates over the existence of a unique China model, different from the model of Japan and that of the Four Asian Tigers and other success stories in the history of economic development. Not only has the participation of Chinese firms in GVCs brought about an export miracle; it has also accelerated China's industrialization, which eventually fueled China's sustained high economic growth over the last four decades. The scope and scale of Chinese firms' participation in GVCs, and the economic consequences of that involvement, are unparalleled. Riding on GVCs to achieve economic growth and industrialization is a unique feature of the China model. However, GVC involvement is not risk-free. Natural disasters and geo-political tensions can disrupt the smooth operations and reliability of value chains. The ongoing US–China trade war has artificially raised the cost of sourcing products from China for the US market. As the trade war has evolved into a technology war, the Trump administration had barred dozens of Chinese firms, including Huawei, from purchasing core technological parts from American companies. This has jeopardized the supply chains of those Chinese firms and threatened the survival of a few Chinese high-technology firms which have been applying GVC strategy. In addition, the outbreak of the COVID-19 pandemic not only disrupted Chinese supply chains, crucial to the operation of foreign upstream firms but also exposed the vulnerability inherent in excessive reliance of many countries on China for supply of the medical goods desperately needed for fighting the pandemic. The trade war and the COVID-19 pandemic have prompted some MNCs to shift their production facilities out of China. It is quite likely that the trend will continue and will eventually reshape China-centered GVCs and steer the future trajectory of GVCs in general.

Chapter 2

Overview: China's Export Miracle, 1980–2018

China's export miracle began unfolding in the 1980s, after the Chinese government determined to launch its revolutionary economic reforms and to open China's doors to the rest of the world. This marked a paradigm shift in the trajectory of Chinese economic development: from a centrally planned economy to a market-oriented one; from autarky to an open economy. The economic reforms and the accompanying open-door policy have transformed the Chinese economy from a virtually closed economy into the largest trading nation in the world and the global center of manufacturing. As a result, made in China products, ranging from cheap and labor-intensive goods such as shoes, apparel, textiles and toys, to high value, high-technology products including TVs, refrigerators, personal computers and smartphones, have penetrated almost every corner of the global market.

Before China set out on its new journey, the Chinese government had not considered international trade a source of economic growth. In the mindsets of the Chinese officials, there was no concept of international division of labor; on the contrary, "independence and self-reliance" were promoted as a central principle of the national development strategy. In accordance with this principle, the Chinese government officials drafted economic development plans detailing what Chinese firms should produce, and how much;

what Chinese households could consume, and how much; and at what prices production inputs and consumer goods should be traded. The centrally planned economic system was supposed to bring wealth and economic prosperity to the Chinese people; in the end, this system failed in China, just as it did in the former Soviet Union and the Eastern European countries that adopted it after World War II.

The revolutionary economic reforms and open-door policy saved the Chinese economy when it was on the verge of collapse, and prompted its integration into the world economy; brought tremendous prosperity and wealth to the Chinese people; and transformed China into the world's second largest economy, rivaling the US. In the last four decades, the explosive growth of Chinese exports was one of the most important engines driving the Chinese economy forward. Following in the footsteps of Japan and the Four Asian Tigers — Korea, Hong Kong, Singapore and Taiwan — which have successfully grown into high-income economies by pursuing export-oriented growth strategy, China has achieved rapid industrialization and unprecedented economic growth by taking advantage of international trade. The dramatic expansion of Chinese exports in the global market is even more impressive than that of Japan and the Four Asian Tigers. First, China emerged as the world's leading exporting nation in 2009 when it was far from an industrialized country status and its per capita GDP was less than $4,000; second, Chinese exports have come to dominate the world market not only in labor-intensive goods but also in high value-added technology products; finally, in less than 30 years China has moved from virtual isolation from the rest of the world to the recognition as the largest exporting nation in the world. China's quick rise as a leading exporter in the world economy is an extraordinary, indeed unprecedented, miracle.

In this chapter, I briefly present some stylized facts related to the Chinese export miracle, focusing on the growth of Chinese exports, the importance of this growth to the Chinese economy and the evolution underlying China's rise as a dominant player in world trade. Countries export different types of goods at different stages of economic development, with low-income countries producing resource- and labor-intensive products, eventually moving up the product ladder in terms of technology and skills as their average incomes rise. Four decades is a long enough period for the examination of the dynamic changes in Chinese export structure. To illustrate the evolution of Chinese industrial specialization in the world economy, I analyze the dynamic changes in Chinese export structure in terms of the distribution of exports among agriculture, resources, and labor- and technology-intensive products. Particular attention is paid to the rise of China as a leading high-technology exporting nation.

The US is the largest single market in the world economy; it is also the most open and competitive market. Countries pursuing export-oriented growth strategy generally place the highest priority on penetration of the US market. The seemingly insatiable American consumer demand for imports offers unparalleled opportunities for those nations to increase their income, simply by increasing their exports to the US. To date, trade with the US is China's most important bilateral trade; China ships more than one-fifth of its exports to the US market and derives more than half of its trade surplus there. Growth in Chinese exports to the US is a major element of China's export miracle. The prevalence of made in China goods in the US market is clearly a significant dimension of China's rise as a dominant exporting nation. To augment the aforementioned discussion of China's export miracle, in this chapter, I also examine China–US trade relations over the period 1980–2018, focusing on the growth of Chinese exports to the US, the bilateral trade balance and trade in advanced technology products (ATPs).

What could account for the rise of China in global trade? Various strands of the literature have presented theoretical explanations centered on causes such as comparative advantage; China's domestic institutional reforms; the exchange rate regime; inflows of FDI; China's accession to the WTO; unprecedented trade liberalization. At the end of the chapter, I briefly review the range of interpretations of China's remarkable success in exports along the aforementioned dimensions. Xing and Detert (2010) identified the failure of conventional trade statistics to accurately measure contemporary bilateral trade balances and actual export capacity of national economies; subsequently economists have adopted trade in value added as an alternative to the evaluation of bilateral trade balances; trade in value added is now a popular quantitative measure of global value chain (GVC) participation by national economies. The arguments in this chapter are grounded solely on conventional trade statistics for discussion of the performance of Chinese exports, and use of gross value rather than value added to analyze the rise of China in global trade, since the concept of trade in value added is native to the GVC phenomenon. I leave Chapter 3 for the discussion of the role of GVCs in the fostering of China's export miracle and the evaluation of China's value-added exports.

China's export miracle: 1980–2018

Figure 2.1 illustrates the growth of Chinese exports and its relative importance to the Chinese economy. The bar graph presents volume of annual Chinese exports in current US dollars from 1980 to 2018, while the line graph shows the trend in the exports to GDP ratio, which measures the relative importance of exports to the Chinese economy. The data were retrieved from the World Trade

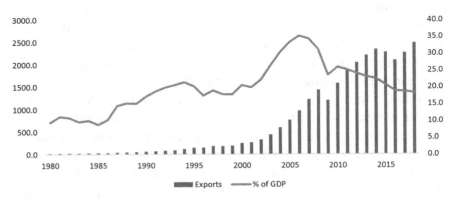

Figure 2.1   China's exports to the world: 1980–2018 (Billion US dollar)

Source: The WTO and the World Bank.

Organization (WTO) and the World Bank database. In 1980, China exported $18.2 billion in goods to the rest of the world; by 2000, that yearly figure had surged to $249.2 billion, more than 10 times the figure at the beginning of the 1980s, representing an average annual growth of 14 percent, much higher than China's GDP growth during the same period. From 2000 onward, the growth of Chinese exports accelerated, exceeding 20 percent each year during the decade 2000–2010. By 2010, China's exports had reached a new high of $1.58 trillion, the largest in the world. Two years later, Chinese exports rose to over $2 trillion: China was the first nation in the history of the world economy to export more than $2 trillion in a single year. In the three-decade period 1980–2010, Chinese exports consistently grew much faster than the Chinese economy and contributed significantly to its economic growth. The rapid expansion of Chinese exports in the global market not only raised the income of Chinese households but also supported the domestic investment indispensable for continuous expansion of the economy. The importance of exports to the Chinese economy can be seen from China's exports to GDP ratio. In 1980, exports were less than one-tenth of Chinese GDP; by 2006, they had jumped to 35.2 percent, suggesting that the dependence of the Chinese economy on external demand had deepened tremendously.

As China grew to become a major trading nation in the world economy, its share of world exports increased continuously. Figure 2.2 shows the evolution of the relative weight of Chinese exports in world trade from 1980 to 2018, compared with those of Japan, Germany and the US. At the beginning of the 1980s, China was a marginal player in world trade. Its merchandise export volume was less than one percent of world exports. Despite China's rapid growth in the 1980s and 1990s, its share of global trade remained moderate; in 2000 China accounted for a mere 3.9 percent of world exports. The explosive growth of Chinese exports after China's official accession to the WTO significantly raised the status of China in world trade. In 2004, China's share of world exports rose to 6.4 percent; China by then outperformed Japan (the largest Asian economy at the time), and was the third largest exporting

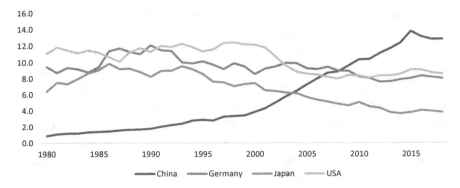

Figure 2.2   Merchandise exports of China, Germany, Japan and the US (As percentage of world exports)

Source: Author's calculation based on the WTO data.

nation in the world. Three years later, China achieved another milestone: for the first time in history, China exported more goods than the US, the largest economy in the world. Given that the Chinese economy was less than half the size of the US economy, China's surpassing of the US and emerging as the second largest exporter were a stunning development. Just five years later, in 2009, the volume of Chinese exports made up 9.6 percent of world exports, exceeding the share of Germany and making China the largest exporting nation in the world. By 2018, China's share soared to 12.8 percent, almost 5 percentage points higher than that of the US, whose economy was then 30 percent larger than China's.

Dynamic changes in China's export structure

Not only did the volume of Chinese exports increase tremendously, the structure of Chinese exports also underwent a dramatic transformation. The share of high value and relatively technologically sophisticated products among China's exports increased dramatically, while those of agriculture and resource- and labor-intensive products dropped substantially. Table 2.1 shows the distribution of Chinese exports among agriculture, fuels and minerals, and

Table 2.1   Structure of Chinese exports in 1990 and 2018 (As percentage of total Chinese exports)

Merchandise	1990	2018
Agricultural products	16.2	3.3
Fuels and mining products	10.6	3.2
Manufactured goods	71.4	93.2
Machinery and transport equipment	17.4	48.6
Textiles	11.6	4.8
Clothing	15.6	6.3
Telecommunications equipment	4.2	12.7
Electronic data processing and office equipment	0.6	8.8

Source: Calculations by the author based on data from the WTO database.

manufactured products in 1990 and 2018. For an examination of changes in specialization within manufacturing, it also lists the shares of machinery and transportation equipment, textiles, clothing, telecommunications equipment, and electronic data processing and office equipment, which comprise the bulk of manufacturing exports. In 1990, China's export specialization was consistent with the classic theory of comparative advantage, which explains trade as the result of differences between national factor supplies, or labor productivity. Agricultural products accounted for 16.2 percent of Chinese exports, while fuels and mining products totaled 10.6 percent. Textiles and clothing accounted for 11.6 and 15.6 percent, respectively. Agriculture, fuels and mining are intensive users of land and mineral reserves, whereas textiles and clothing are intensive users of low-skilled labor. In 1990, resource- and labor-intensive goods constituted more than half of Chinese exports.

Between 1990 and 2018, China's export pattern changed substantially. In 2018, manufactured goods dominated Chinese exports, with a 93 percent share, while the aggregate share of agriculture, fuels and mining products dropped below 7 percent. China has become a net oil importer since the mid-1990s. It is not surprising to see this fall in the share of fuels and mining products among Chinese exports: with the world's largest manufacturing output, especially in a few resource-intensive products such as steel and aluminum, China has become the largest importer of a number of mineral resources. The dominance of manufactured products indicates that Chinese exports have fully migrated from agriculture- and resource-oriented specialization — the initial stage where low-income countries enter international trade — to manufacturing specialization.

Within the manufacturing sector, Chinese exports experienced a pronounced shift away from labor-intensive products such as textiles and clothing, toward high-value, relatively skill-intensive products: machinery and transport equipment, telecommunications equipment, and electronic data processing and office equipment. Between 1990 and 2018, the share of machinery and transport equipment in China's exports jumped from 17.4 percent to 48.6 percent; the share of electronic data processing and office equipment (mainly personal computers and handheld tablets) rose from less than one percent to 8.8 percent; and that of telecommunications equipment such as mobile phones increased from 4.2 percent to 12.7 percent. The shares of both textiles and clothing fell sharply, to 4.8 percent and 6.3 percent, respectively. To a certain extent, the transition from resource- and labor-intensive products to skill-intensive products indicates that Chinese exports are climbing further up the ladder of industrial specialization.

The fact that China has emerged as the world's largest maker of toys and exporter of textile products should not surprise its trading partners. China's rich endowment of labor, along with a seemingly unlimited supply of rural labor released from the agriculture sector, gave China the comparative advantage in the manufacture of labor-intensive products. As its economy has been gradually integrated into the world economy, China is naturally evolving as a major exporter in almost all categories of labor-intensive products, including shoes, travel gear, clothing and toys. If a country were to specialize in producing low value-added, labor-intensive commodities forever, free trade would be a curse rather than a blessing for that country. This is actually one of the major points on which developing countries are suspicious of free trade. In the case of China, economic integration into the global economy has not only greatly expanded the utilization of China's abundant human resources and augmented its specialization in labor-intensive production but it has also facilitated the development of Chinese capacity to manufacture high value-added products, which in turn is inducing fundamental changes in the country's trade structure.

The rapid growth of Chinese exports of high-technology products highlights another aspect of the Chinese export miracle: the shift of Chinese export specialization out of resource- and low-skilled, labor-intensive products. High-technology products, defined as goods with high research and development intensity, include aerospace equipment, computers, pharmaceuticals, scientific instruments and electrical machinery. As a low-income developing country, China was a marginal exporter of high-technology products until 2000, but by 2007 it had emerged as the leading high-technology exporting nation, surpassing the US, Japan, and the 27 EU countries (Meri, 2009). Figure 2.3 depicts the annual high-technology export volumes of China, Japan, Germany and the US from 2007 to 2017. It reveals a few surprising facts. First, China's high-technology export volume had for some time been much

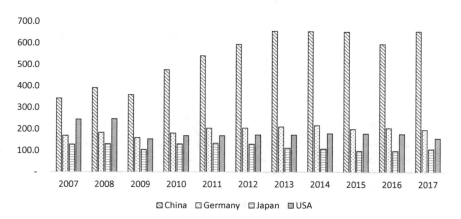

Figure 2.3 China: The leading high-technology exporting nation (Billion US dollar)

Source: The World Bank.

higher than that of Japan, Germany or the US. Second, China's high technology exports rose to $654.2 billion, almost double the figure for 2007. In contrast, the high-technology exports of the US, the undisputable world leader in science and technology, decreased to $156.9 billion in 2017, two-third of the figure for 2007, while the exports of Japan and Germany were either stagnant or grew only moderately over the same period. It is important to emphasize that in 2007, China's GDP per capita was $3,800, less than one-tenth of that of Japan, Germany or the US. It is almost beyond imagining, that a developing country could be an exporter of capital- and technology-intensive products, not to mention a leading high-technology export-ing nation. China's impressive achievement in high-technology exports is a remarkable phenomenon bordering on the miraculous.

While Chinese exports have diversified into capital- and tech-nology-intensive products, China's dominance in the world market of labor-intensive products such as textiles and clothing products has not weakened, in fact it has grown even stronger. Figure 2.4 displays the shares of Chinese made textiles, clothing, electronic data processing and office equipment, and telecommunications

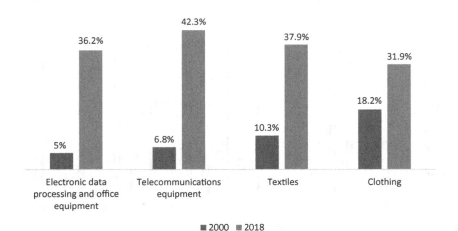

Figure 2.4   Exports for which China was the world top exporter (Percentage of world exports in each category)

Source: The author's calculations, based on the WTO data.

equipment in world exports of these products. These product categories are the ones where China ranked as the world's largest exporter. In 2000, China's share in world exports of telecommunications equipment, mostly mobile phones, was only 6.8 percent. That figure rose significantly, surging to 42.3 percent by 2018, showing the dominance of Chinese-made telecommunications equipment in the world market. Similarly, in 2000 Chinese exports were a relatively small element of world exports of electronic data processing and office equipment, including computers, fax machines, and printers, contributing about 5 percent of world exports in that category. Since then, China's market share increased steadily, in 2018 reaching 36.2 percent of world electronic data processing and office equipment exports. Those two groups of products were the largest contributors to the boom in Chinese high-technology exports. The rapid expansion of high-technology products among Chinese exports, however, did not constrain the expansion of China in the global market for labor-intensive products. China's share of the global textiles and clothing markets also increased impressively in the same period. In 2000, China accounted for 10.3 percent of world textile exports and 18.2 percent of world clothing exports; by 2018, China's share in textiles jumped to 37.9 percent, in clothing to 31.9 percent. The 2005 abolition of the Multifiber Arrangement, which used quotas to limit the access of China's exports to international markets for those product types, removed institutional barriers, and greatly boosted the growth of Chinese exports in those categories.

China's trade with the US

The US is the largest and most liberal market in the world. It has the lowest tariff and non-tariff barriers to foreign goods; thus it is the most competitive market. For countries pursuing export-led growth strategy and relying on external demand, the US market is the prime destination market for their products. Made in China goods have successfully penetrated the US market, which is now the largest overseas market for Chinese exports. Every year, more than

Table 2.2   China's commodity trade with the US, 1980–2018 (Billion US dollar)

Year	Exports	Surplus	Percentage of US trade deficit
1980	1.1	−2.7	N/A
1990	15.2	10.4	10.3
2000	100.1	83.8	19.2
2005	243.5	202.3	26.2
2010	365.0	273.0	43.0
2015	483.2	367.3	49.3
2018	539.7	419.5	48.0

Source: US Census Bureau and the author's calculations.

one-fifth of Chinese exports find their way to the US market. The remarkable success of made in China goods in the US is another facet of China's export miracle.

Table 2.2 provides an overview of the evolution of Chinese exports to the US from 1980 to 2018. Here I use data published by the US Census Bureau rather than Chinese Customs, mainly because a substantial portion of Chinese goods enter the US indirectly, from entrepots outside of Mainland China. For instance, billions of dollars in Chinese goods are shipped to the US from Hong Kong every year. Chinese Customs records these goods as exports to Hong Kong, while US Customs books them as imports from China, in accordance with rules of origin followed by WTO members. The data from the US Census Bureau provide a more accurate description of the evolution of the US market for made in China products.

In 1980, China exported $1.1 billion in goods to the US, less than 0.5 percent of US total imports. By 2000, China's exports to the US had jumped almost one hundred-fold, to $100.1 billion, accounting for about 8 percent of total US imports. It took China 20 years to achieve its first $100 billion in exports to the US. Chinese exports to the US went on to increase even more dramatically, gaining an extraordinarily large share of the US market. In 2018, China exported $540 billion in goods to the US, more than five times the figure for 2000, accounting for more than 20 percent of total US imports from all its trading partners.

As Chinese exports to the US continued to rise dramatically, China's trade surplus with the US widened accordingly. Even more importantly, China was by then the single most important source of the tremendous US trade deficit. Table 2.2 also presents China's trade surplus with the US from 1980 to 2018. Actually, in 1980 China had a $2.7 billion trade deficit with the US. Because of the exponential growth of China's exports to the US in the following decades, by 1990 China had a $10.4 billion trade surplus with the US, roughly one-tenth of the US trade deficit. China's trade surplus with the US had risen dramatically since then, surging to $83.8 billion in 2000, to $273 billion in 2010. By 2018, the trade surplus had skyrocketed to $419.5 billion. As a consequence, almost half of the US trade deficit could be traced back to trade with China. To a certain extent, the excessive concentration of the US trade deficit in China mirrors the competitiveness of made in China goods against American goods and those from other countries. On the other hand, compared with the share of the Chinese economy in the world economy, the share of China in the US trade deficit is disproportionally high, which implies that China's comparative advantage, institutional reforms, and trade liberalization provide only a very limited explanation for the deficit, and actually present more puzzles regarding the extraordinary performance of made in China goods in the US.

One particular phenomenon within China–US trade deserves special attention: China's positioning as a net exporter to the US of high-technology goods. Given China's huge population and low income relative to those of the US, it is not surprising to Americans that China specializes in low value, labor-intensive products in its trade with the US. It is normal for American consumers to see cheap, labor-intensive products, such as apparel, shoes, footwear, toys, consumer electronics, textiles and accessories, flooding the US market. The China–US trade pattern in the 1980s and 1990s appears to be consistent with China's comparative advantage in labor intensive industry (Morrison, 2018).

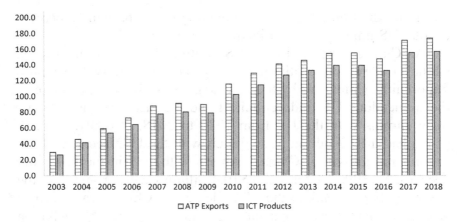

Figure 2.5   China's trade with the US in ATPs (Billion US dollar)
Source: US Census Bureau.

However, as the world entered the 21st century, China dramatically diversified its product lines and gradually moved into high value products. Specifically, its exports to the US in ATPs expanded rapidly. Figure 2.5 shows the trend in Chinese ATP exports to the US during the period 2003–2018, based on data retrieved from the US Census Bureau. According to the US Census Bureau, ATP is defined as a composite of 10 groups of technology products: (1) biotechnology, (2) life sciences, (3) opto-electronics, (4) information and communication, (5) electronics, (6) flexible manufacturing, (7) advanced materials, (8) aerospace, (9) weapons and (10) nuclear technology. At the beginning of the 2000s, China's ATP exports to the US were moderate. In 2003, China exported $29.4 billion in ATPs to the US, about 14 percent of US imports in that category. The volume of Chinese exports increased sharply, jumping to $173.8 billion in 2018, more than five times that in 2003 and exceeding one third of total Chinese exports to the US and accounting for 35 percent of total US ATP imports from the world.

The composition structure of Chinese ATP exports shows that information and communications technology (ICT), largely personal computers, mobile phones, digital cameras and handheld tablets, was the main source of the growth. In 2003, ICT made up 89 percent of Chinese ATP exports to the US. That percentage changed very little from 2003 to 2018. In 2018, the US imported $157.1 billion in ICT from China, accounting for about 90 percent of Chinese ATP exports to the US. Without a doubt, classic trade theories emphasizing labor productivity, resource endowment and economies of scale, cannot explain why a developing country like China has consistently run a huge ATP trade surplus with the US, the world's leading nation in science and technology.

Conventional explanations of the Chinese export miracle

Scholars and China watchers have taken a variety of approaches in their attempts to identify the factors contributing to the Chinese export miracle of the last four decades. Numerous articles on these issues have been published in academic journals, magazines and newspapers. The first, perhaps most obvious, explanation for China's export miracle is its comparative advantage in labor-intensive products. According to the Ricardian comparative theory, China has a significantly lower opportunity cost than advanced nations in the production of labor-intensive products. In line with the Heckscher–Ohlin theory based on resource endowments, China, being the world's most populous country, and being endowed with a massive body of cheap labor, even enjoyed a comparative advantage over other developing nations. China's comparative advantage in labor-intensive products is regarded as one of the major factors driving its extraordinary growth and the worldwide expansion of its exports (Adams *et al.*, 2006; Wang, 2006).

A second explanation lies in China's series of institutional reforms — particularly the decentralization of its once highly centralized international trade system and the reform of foreign trade enterprises through the introduction of incentive mechanisms — all of which prompted the flourishing of foreign trade companies at the provincial and municipal levels, and motivated firms engaged in foreign trade to expand their export capacity (Hu and Khan, 1997; Lin *et al.*, 2003; Lardy, 2003).

A third factor explaining the remarkable expansion of made in China products in the world market is the considerable improvement of market access for Chinese products through institutional arrangements (WTO membership, bilateral and multilateral free trade agreements, and the abolition of the Multifiber Arrangement). The accession to the WTO enabled China to receive most favorable nation treatment, which has enhanced the access of Chinese goods to foreign markets. The apparel and textile industries enjoyed massive gains following the abolition of the Multifiber Arrangement, which had limited China's exports (Branstetter and Lardy, 2006; Prasad, 2009; Wakasugi and Zhang, 2015).

Two more factors, devaluation of the yuan and pegging to the dollar regime, are argued to have been largely influential in strengthening the competitiveness of made in China products. The Chinese yuan had been on a devaluation track since 1980. Yuan devaluations until 1989 simply corrected the yuan's over-valuation under the centrally planned economy; subsequent devaluations may have undervalued the yuan, enhancing the global competitiveness of Chinese exports. From then until 2005 the yuan was pegged to the dollar. There are still debates as to whether the Chinese government deliberately used the devaluation of the yuan to boost its exports, and whether a series of yuan devaluations did in fact strengthen the competitiveness of Chinese goods in international markets (Naughton, 1996; Marquez and Schindler, 2007; Thorbecke and Smith, 2010).

Finally, massive inflows of export-oriented FDI have greatly expanded China's export capacity. The Chinese government's preferential policies regarding export-oriented FDI (including corporate tax reductions, readily available land for the construction of factories, and exemption from tariffs on imported machines and production materials) attracted many foreign MNCs to use China as an export platform; this dramatically raised China's export capacity for a variety of products (Zhang and Song, 2000; Whalley and Xin, 2010).

Conclusion

In less than 30 years, China evolved from a closed, centrally planned economy to the largest exporting nation in the world. It now dominates the world market, not only in labor-intensive products such as textiles and clothing, which is consistent with its comparative advantage as the most populous developing country, but also in capital and skill-intensive high-technology products, such as smartphones, personal computers and digital cameras, which were invented and developed in industrialized countries. In terms of bilateral trade, China accounted for 20 percent of the US imports, and almost half of the US trade deficit originated from China. Even more surprising, the US, the undisputable world leader in science and technology, incurred a huge trade deficit with China in ATPs. By any standard, China's rise as a leading exporting nation is an unprecedented miracle.

Many theories offer explanations for the Chinese miracle, from different perspectives, including classic comparative advantage theory, FDI theory, arguments focusing on exchange rate regime, trade liberalization, and institutional reforms, but no single theory can fully account for China's emergence as the world No. 1 trading nation. When China first surpassed Japan and the US and emerged as the leading high technology exporter, China was a developing country with per capita GDP of less than $4,000. A few years later, when China took the title of world's largest exporting nation away from Germany, long famous for its automobile and machinery industry, China was still far from completing its transition to industrialized country status. These intriguing developments require new theories beyond conventional wisdoms for a complete elucidation of the Chinese miracle. In the next chapter, I investigate the Chinese export miracle from the largely unexplored perspective of GVCs, which offers answers to many of the questions still surrounding the Chinese miracle.

Chapter 3

GVCs: Catalyst of the Explosive Growth of China's Exports

In Chapter 2, I briefly summarized China's remarkable achievements in exports over the last four decades. The story of the explosive expansion of China's exports is by any standard unprecedented in the history of the world economy. China led the world in exports of not only low-skilled and labor-intensive goods but also skill-intensive technology products. Despite China's obvious technology gaps with developed countries, the sophistication of China's exports almost matches that of the leaders. What could account for China's export boom? How have made in China products become so competitive and popular in the global market? What were the major forces driving that worldwide expansion?

With a population of more than 1.4 billion, China is clearly endowed with comparative advantage in labor-intensive products. Without doubt, since the 1990s market access for Chinese exports has improved substantially, thanks to trade liberalization in terms of tariff reductions, and trade facilitation, in particular China's entry into the World Trade Organization (WTO) and the abolition of the Multifiber Arrangement. The arguments surrounding comparative advantage and the under-valued yuan are focused on the cost advantage of Chinese exports, while trade liberalization and domestic institutional reforms are concerned with the importance of freedom to conduct trade and an environment conducive to Chinese exports.

These popular explanations of China's success basically assume that the competitiveness of made in China products is determined by China's intrinsic comparative advantage; that competition in international markets is between made in China and not made in China products; and that Chinese firms enter global markets independently and compete either with local firms or with firms from third countries. They fail to take into consideration the organizational changes in production and international trade induced by the development of global value chains (GVCs), where Chinese exporting firms have performed only tasks necessary for the delivery of final products to consumers in international markets.

In the classic models of Ricardo and Heckscher–Ohlin, comparative advantage is the sole factor determining competitiveness and trade patterns. Today's trade, however, is not cloth for wine: the proliferation of GVCs has seen trade in goods replaced by trade in tasks (Grossman and Rossi-Hansberg, 2008), where a number of firms in diverse geographic locations jointly deliver ready-to-use products to consumers in the global market. The comparative advantage of an individual country cannot decide the competitiveness of products manufactured and traded along GVCs. Chinese-made manufacturing products, which account for more than 90 percent of the national exports, are mostly produced and manufactured along value chains led by foreign multinational corporations (MNCs). The brands, technology, and global distribution and retail networks owned by GVC lead firms are critical means of overcoming barriers to market entry, and hence to determining the winners and losers in international markets.

For instance, in the casual fashion market, competition is not between made in China and not made in China apparel; rather, competition is between different brands, for example GAP vs. UNIQLO; in the personal computer market, it is not competition between made in China and made in Japan personal computers, but between DELL and HP; in the retail market, competition is not between made in China goods and locally made goods, it is between retail chains such as Walmart and Target, both of whom source billions of dollars in products from China.

GVCs are particularly relevant to Chinese exports, as about half of its manufacturing exports were assembled with imported parts and components, and most of the so-called made in China products available in international markets either carry brands owned by foreign MNCs or are distributed by global retail giants such as Walmart. In this chapter, I analyze China's export boom in the context of GVCs, and argue that GVCs have served as a vehicle for Chinese exports' entry into international markets, especially markets in high income countries. By successfully plugging into GVCs, Chinese firms have been able to bundle their low-skilled labor services with globally recognized brands and/or the advanced technologies of MNCs, and thereby selling those labor services to consumers in global markets. Continuous technology innovation, aggressive promotion of brands and the worldwide development of distribution networks by GVC lead firms constantly create new markets and raise consumer demand for a variety of products, and hence increase demand for made in China goods or tasks performed by the Chinese firms involved in those value chains, eventually stimulating China's export activity.

The integration of Chinese firms into GVCs has been a catalyst for the sustained high growth of Chinese exports over the last four decades. If we examine the situation from the GVC perspective, we can easily see why China, a developing country which under the classical theory is expected to export labor-intensive or low-skilled products, in fact exports high-technology products to developed countries; why China is the leading athletic shoe exporter even though it does not have an internationally recognized athletic shoe brand yet; and why relatively low productivity Chinese firms can export their products to the most competitive markets, such as the US and Japan.

To demonstrate the critical role of GVCs in powering the explosive growth of Chinese exports in the last four decades, I begin with a theoretical explanation of how participation in GVCs could boost China's exports. The theoretical analysis, focusing on three spillover effects of GVCs, involving brands, technology and product innovation, and the distribution and retail networks of GVC lead firms, is followed by an analysis of how those spillover effects have facilitated the expansion of Chinese exports to global markets. Then, I quantify the linkage between Chinese exports and GVCs and discuss how Chinese exports benefit from the three spillover effects.

GVCs are a micro-phenomenon. Aggregated data provide an outline of the overall picture of a national economy's participation in GVCs, but do not elucidate the specific roles and functions of firms involved, which are critical for an understanding of the evolution of and rationale for GVCs in the world economy. As pointed out by Gereffi *et al.* (2005), the relationships between the lead firms and downstream suppliers along value chains determine the contribution and importance of GVCs in terms of trade promotion and technology spillovers. To investigate the specific participation of Chinese firms in GVCs and the dependence of Chinese exports on GVC spillover effects, I first identify the tasks performed by the Chinese firms in the creation of specific products, then expand the scope of the analysis to industrial scale, and finally to Chinese exports in general. Specifically, I begin with a discussion of the exports of iPhones and laptop computers, and then extend the discussion to high-technology products, a sector where China has emerged as the topmost exporter in the world.

How to quantify the GVC participation of a national economy remains an open question. Instead of adopting the GVC participation index introduced by the Organisation for Economic Co-operation and Development (OECD), I rely mainly on the ratio of processing exports in Chinese exports as an indicator of the minimum dependence of Chinese exports on GVCs. Processing exports are a subset of GVC activities. Processing exports reveal the tasks performed by Chinese firms, and also provide a direct measure of exports associated with GVC participation. I use Chinese customs statistics on processing exports within high-technology and bilateral trade to directly quantify the participation of Chinese firms in value chains. At the end of this chapter, I explain why the share of processing exports is a more accurate measure of the reliance of Chinese exports on GVCs than the GVC participation index, even at the aggregate level. In addition, a large portion of Chinese exports, such as shoes, toys, apparel, furniture and accessories, are manufactured for global brand vendors such as H&M, ZARA and UNIQLO, and for large retailers. These exports generally contain zero foreign value added or imported intermediate inputs. The Chinese firms supplying these products are definitely part of value chains operated by global brand vendors and retailers. That kind of exports unambiguously belongs to value chain trade. In the age of GVCs, global brand vendors and large retailers play an important role in international trade: they have built global retail infrastructures for the distribution of goods supplied by their contract manufacturers; this is a case where a spillover effect related to distribution and retail networks effectively promotes the access of Chinese goods to foreign markets. On the other hand, processing exports require foreign intermediate inputs. Using share of processing exports as a proxy for China's participation in GVCs underestimates the actual dependence of Chinese exports on GVCs, as do the GVC participation indices. Proposing a means of compensating for that deficiency, this chapter also discusses the role of large retailers such as Walmart in the promotion of exports of Chinese goods.

Spillover effects of GVCs

GVCs, a new form of business operation, involve multiple countries in the creation of goods and delivery of those goods to end consumers in international markets. Production fragmentation and modularization enable highly efficient production processes for the distribution of ready-to-use goods, particularly information and communications technology (ICT), to geographically dispersed locations. In recent decades, the main drivers of the emergence of GVCs have been unprecedented liberalization of trade and investment; innovation in marine transportation; and the profit seeking behavior of MNCs (Baldwin, 2016). Today, most manufacturing commodities are produced and traded along value chains. A typical GVC orchestrates the performance of a series of tasks necessary for the delivery of a product. From conception to delivery to the end consumer, these tasks include research and development, product design, manufacture of parts and components, and assembly and distribution (Gereffi and Karina, 2011). Firms in different countries complete those tasks in a highly coordinated manner. Each firm specializes in one or more tasks in which it has comparative advantage, and contributes part of the total value added of the final product. GVCs represent a new international division of labor in tasks contributing to the production and delivery of a single product. Compared to conventional specialization at the product level, specialization in tasks along value chains is a refined process involving division of labor among nations that enhances resource allocation efficiency and raises the productivity and economic growth of all economies involved.

The spillover effects benefiting non-lead firms along a value chain are dependent on the presence of a lead firm that manages the operations of the value chain and decides the relations between the firms participating in the chain. A lead firm, which may be a technology leader, a brand marketer or a larger retailer, plays a central role in organizing all the tasks of a GVC, including product design, the outsourcing of manufacturing activities, product distribution and retailing. Generally, if we break down the tasks contributing to the production of a product, from supplying of the required raw materials to manufacturing of the product and on to the eventual delivery of the product to targeted consumers, we can easily sketch a chain that superficially links all of the firms involved in the process. However, if the links along a value chain are not bound by contracts, i.e., if the relations are simply defined by free market transactions as buyer–seller relations, the value chain will generate few spillover effects to the participating non-lead firms. A value chain without a lead firm, or one where the relations between firms are simply market based and not bound by contracts, generates little externality for its participating firms, in particular those from developing countries. Gereffi *et al.* (2005) identify five different types of relationships in value chains. Between the two extreme cases (vertically integrated firms and market-based relations) there are three governance structures: modular, relational and captive (where a lead firm is necessary for the management of relations and for the operations of value chains). GVCs can be classified by governance structure into producer-driven and buyer-driven value chains. GVCs led by technology leaders in capital-intensive industries such as automobiles, aircraft, computers and semiconductors are producer-driven value chains. On the other hand, buyer-driven chains are typically organized by large retailers, branded marketers and branded manufacturers (Gereffi, 1999). The automobile value chains organized by the Japanese automaker Toyota and the iPhone value chain of Apple are producer-driven GVCs. Walmart, taking advantage of its extensive retail networks in the US and other countries, has built its buyer-driven GVC by sourcing all goods from contract manufacturers.

Below I discuss spillover effects of GVCs at the micro-level and discuss the ways in which spillover effects have helped Chinese firms overcome barriers to enter into international markets and facilitated their dramatic global expansion. Cheap labor and the so-called undervalued yuan are often cited as comparative advantage of Chinese firms. At first glance, it would seem that as long as firms can manufacture products at competitive prices, they would be able to compete and sell their products in international markets. In fact, competition in international markets is much more complicated than this simple reasoning suggests. Production costs are only one of the many factors determining whether products are attractive to foreign consumers and competitive in international markets. The modularization of manufacturing has lowered barriers to enter into a number of industries. It is relatively easy to produce ready-to-use goods by purchasing standard machines and outsourcing necessary modules — but intangible assets such as brands and global distribution networks are major hurdles for firms in developing countries striving to take part in international markets (Kaplinsky, 2000).

Spillover effect 1: Brands

One of the three main GVC spillover effects has to do with the internationally recognized brands owned by GVC lead firms, whose investment in and promotion of brand development usually generates a positive externality and benefits all firms involved in the related value chains. Brands are one of the critical determinants of consumer choices. Consumers have relatively little information about the materials used in and the quality of products. In that asymmetric information situation, consumers generally regard publicly recognized brands as an assurance of product quality (Bronnenberg *et al.*, 2012). In addition, when consumers face a large array of differentiated products (a common situation in this age of mass production), brands can serve as a means of simplifying routine purchase decisions. When purchasing branded products such as fashion, jewelry, watches and athletic footwear, brand-oriented consumers often choose products that embody the images that they want to project. In the case of electronics and high-technology products, brands proxy for technology trends and frontiers. Luxury good brands are always associated with social prestige (Chipman, 2019). Most consumers, in particular those in developed countries and those from the middle- and higher-income classes in developing countries, tend to be brand oriented and have high willingness to pay for a particular brand. It is very challenging for newcomers, especially firms from developing countries, to enter international markets dominated by established brands. Switching cost tends to undermine consumer willingness to replace preferred brands with new alternatives. Consumer bias toward particular brands grants an advantage to incumbent producers and raises barriers for new entries. Branded products can confidently charge their clients rather high premiums, so low prices often fail to deliver comparative advantage in the markets where brand orientation is prevalent (Credit Suisse, 2010).

Branded clothing constituted the largest share, around 80 percent, of the European clothing market: only 20 percent of clothing was private labels and non-branded items (Thelle, 2012). Nike and Adidas almost monopolize the global athletic shoe market. In 2018, Nike, who also owns Converse, occupied 42 percent of the $58 billion athletic shoe market; Adidas 26 percent. Together the two companies controlled more than two-thirds of the market (Russell, 2019).

Despite more than four decades of high growth, Chinese firms have not nurtured a significant number of globally recognized brands. In 2019, Huawei was the only Chinese brand on the global brand chart. Even though China is the world's largest exporter of shoes, there is no Chinese brand among the top 10 global shoe makers. Creating and sustaining global brands requires lavish advertising budgets and global promotion campaigns, which are far beyond the capacity of most Chinese firms in the early stages of their development. Moreover, brand images are strongly linked with culture; French perfume, Italian fashion, Japanese cars and Swiss watches are *de facto* regarded as high quality, fashionable products. Cultural stereotyping makes it even more difficult for Chinese firms to market their home-grown brands abroad.

Buyer-driven value chains are usually led by owners of global brands. Popular fashion brands H&M, ZARA, UNIQLO and GAP are all lead firms of buyer-driven value chains. In the personal computer and handheld tablet sectors, Dell, HP, iPad, Kindle and Samsung currently dominate the international market. Those brand marketers, who generally use their monopoly power over their brands to organize value chains, establish worldwide distribution networks and market products globally, employ hundreds of contract manufacturers in China. By plugging into buyer-driven value chains as assemblers or original equipment manufacturers (OEMs), Chinese contract manufacturers are able to bypass brand-related obstacles and take advantage of consumer preferences for international brands, exporting their products under famous foreign brands. In that way, brand-driven demand in international markets automatically translates into demand for made in China products. Unlike non-branded products at equal or lower cost, international brand labels strengthen the competitiveness of made in China products and enhance their appeal to foreign consumers, greatly facilitating their access to international markets and driving the remarkable growth of Chinese exports — even though Chinese firms manufacturing products for brand owners contribute nothing to brand promotion and development. Their exports, however, have risen along with the popularity of the brands owned by GVC lead firms. For instance, as a brand such as UNIQLO becomes popular in more and more countries, made in China products with UNIQLO labels enter more and more foreign markets. The brand spillover effect is a main externality that has helped Chinese exports enter international markets.

Spillover effect 2: Technology and product innovation

The second spillover effect of GVCs is related to technology and product innovation by lead firms of GVCs. Innovation generally gives rise to new products or new models with improved functionality and technology, which in turn give a birth to new markets or boost demand for new models. To a large extent, new and fast growing markets have been nurtured by the technology and product inventions of MNCs, which integrate firms from developing countries into their value chains. Revolutionary innovations in ICT have given rise to a variety of new products, notably personal computers, digital cameras, smartphones and handheld tablets, leading to the opening of an array of new markets and the dramatic expansion of consumer demand beyond entrenched traditional commodities. In 2012, ICT goods emerged as one of the top product groups traded globally. World imports of ICT goods rose to $2 trillion, about 11 percent of world merchandise trade, and exceeded imports of traditional commodities such as agricultural goods and motor vehicles (UNCTAD, 2014).

To implement export-led growth strategy, it is crucial for Chinese firms to take part in newly developed markets and benefit from the explosive demand for goods such as laptop computers, smartphones and digital cameras. However, most if not all of the intellectual properties of ICT are owned by MNCs from developed countries. Established MNCs have comparative advantage in high-technology products; Chinese firms do not. Further, constrained by a shortage of essential human resources, insufficient investment in research and development, and a relatively short learning-by-doing history, Chinese firms found that their products, with indigenous technology, were unable to compete with the products of the incumbent technology leaders in international markets.

The global expansion of value chains, on the other hand, offers Chinese firms a short-cut to participation in the market for high-technology products and a means of benefiting from the fast-growing demand for those products, regardless of the intrinsic disadvantages faced by those firms. Newly developed technological products require not only core technological components but also low-technology parts and labor-intensive services. Smartphones, for example, require core components: operating systems, CPUs, memory chips and camera sensors. Barriers to entry to the work of producing such components are high. It is very challenging for Chinese firms to enter and be competent contenders. On the other hand, making a smartphone requires a number of standard parts — batteries, antennas, camera lens filters — and low-skilled services such as testing and assembly. By specializing in low value-added tasks within the value chains of high-technology products, and producing standard components, Chinese firms can join the value creation processes for high-technology products, benefit from access to growing global markets, and grow together with the lead firms who invent and design the products. The unit value added by Chinese firms as a share of the total value of products may be low, but the sheer size of the world market points to potential for huge growth and economies of scale.

As lead firms of GVCs continue to roll out new products and new models, the demand for those new products and models spills over to the demand for tasks performed by Chinese firms involved in those value chains. For instance, the Chinese firm Sunwoda supplied the batteries for the iPhone X. The increase in demand for the iPhone X automatically translates into increased demand for Sunwoda batteries, even though the latter does not advertise to market its products. This is one way Chinese firms involved in value chains can benefit from the spillover effect of the technology and product innovation of GVC lead firms. It is important to keep in mind that the spillover effect discussed here is different from that analyzed in conventional literature on technology and productivity growth. The spillover effect of technology and product innovation along GVCs refers to an opportunity to take part in the fast growing market for high-technology products, where Chinese firms have neither the necessary technology nor any comparative advantage.

Not just firms from developing countries benefit the spillover effect of the innovation activities of GVC lead firms but firms from industrialized countries can benefit too. For example, Japanese electronics company Toshiba had invented a tiny 1.8 inch disk drive, roughly the size of a silver dollar, with five gigabytes of storage, but Toshiba engineers could not conceive of an application for it. At that time, Apple engineers were designing the first iPod music player, so Apple was looking for a small hard drive capable of storing a few hundred songs. In 2001, during a regular Apple visit to Toshiba, Toshiba engineers showed the tiny disk to the chief architect of the iPod, Jonathan Rubinstein. He immediately realized that it was the right device for the iPod, and paid $10 million to Toshiba for the exclusive right to purchase those drives from Toshiba. After the launch of the iPod, all existing MP3 music players soon disappeared from the market. The success of the iPod gave a new life to a disk drive which in the minds of its inventors had no commercial value. As a supplier of Apple, Toshiba benefited tremendously from the spillover effect of the invention of the iPod.

Similarly, in the 1960s Corning Glass invented Gorilla Glass, which is incredibly strong. For some years the company never found a market for Gorilla Glass — until it was adopted for use in the iPhone, a revolutionary 21st century invention. In the process of designing the iPhone, Steve Jobs instructed his team to find a glass cover which was scratch-resistant and had a more elegant look than any plastic. With the help of a friend, Jobs found that Gorilla Glass was the right material for the iPhone (Isaacson, 2011). Because of the iPhone, Gorilla Glass finally found a market and became a major cash cow of Corning Glass. Now, Gorilla Glass had been used in more than 6 billion devices. Clearly, it was Apple's innovative products, the iPod and the iPhone, that brought commercial life to both Toshiba's tiny disk and Corning's Gorilla Glass, making it one of the most valuable spillover effects that a GVC had ever passed on to the firms participating in its value chains.

Spillover effect 3: Distribution and retail networks

The third and most important spillover effect of GVCs is related to the global distribution and retail networks developed by GVC lead firms. Classic trade models typically assume that home country firms sell their products directly to foreign consumers. In reality, wholesalers and retailers actually constitute a bridge between home producers and final consumers abroad, and affect both patterns of trade and welfare gains. Basic marketing and distribution infrastructure are prerequisites for the linking of domestic supply and foreign demand. The links between exporters and overseas buyers are important channels for the diffusion of knowledge and information about consumer preferences (Egan and Mody, 1992). Selling products globally is much more challenging than selling them domestically: it requires extensive distribution and retail networks across continents, the basic infrastructure by means of which goods can access billions of consumers in other nations. Product reputation, product quality, design and post-sale service are prerequisites for wholesalers/retailers to carry products and put them on the shelves of retail outlets. Chinese firms did not have these features when they first entered the world market, so it was a daunting task to persuade existing distributors and retailers to carry made in China goods. Building extensive international retail networks and opening retail outlets such as Apple stores in many countries are very costly, and almost impossible for most Chinese firms, particularly small and medium firms.

Lead firms in all value chains are buyers. They are responsible for marketing and distribution. For firms who do not have their own global distribution networks, joining GVCs can mitigate information deficiencies, reduce transaction costs and facilitate market access. Taking advantage of the spillover effects of GVCs, Chinese firms have not only been able to enter the world market successfully, they have also been freed of concerns regarding the marketing of their products to consumers in geographically dispersed locations. Global retailers such as ZARA, H&M and UNIQLO have hundreds of Chinese suppliers, and they sell their made in China products via their global retail networks, which enhances the access of Chinese goods to international markets and stimulates the growth of Chinese exports.

New-new trade theory (Inomata, 2017), which emphasizes firm heterogeneity, suggests that fixed costs such as the cost of setting up distribution channels, of gaining an understanding of foreign regulations and consumer preferences, and of making commercials for product promotion, generally hinder firms' efforts to export their products to international markets — so that only larger, more productive firms can enter international markets, while less productive firms can only serve local markets. The new-new trade theory makes an unspoken assumption that when a firm exports its products abroad, it should be responsible for all tasks, from research and development to the manufacture of products, to marketing to consumers. However, that assumption does not hold for modern value chain trade, where there is a clear division of labor between lead firms and non-lead firms. Lead firms are responsible for product design, marketing and retailing, while non-lead firms specialize in the production of parts and components and the assembly of final products. Fixed costs are actually shouldered by lead firms. In principle, a contract manufacturer follows the instructions of its lead firm as to the type of goods to be produced and where the products should be shipped, and is not responsible for marketing or retailing at all. Therefore, once Chinese firms plug into GVCs as designated manufacturers or part suppliers, they are free of the financial burden and commercial activities related to selling their products in international markets. They simply sell their products via the distribution and retail networks built up by GVC lead firms.

This third type of GVC spillover effect eliminates the burden of fixed costs emphasized in the new-new trade theory. Some empirical studies report that less productive Chinese firms export larger volumes than more productive firms. Lu (2010) discovered that China's exporters were typically less productive than non-exporters, and sold less in the domestic market. Dai *et al.* (2016) demonstrated that Chinese firms engaged in processing exports were relatively less productive. Malikov *et al.* (2017) examined Chinese firms in 28 industries and found that exporters exhibited lower productivity than non-exporters. The key to solving the productivity puzzle revealed by those studies is the spillover effects of GVCs.

GVCs and the global expansion of China's exports

In this section, I present a few stylized facts to demonstrate the dependence of Chinese exports on GVCs and the importance of GVCs to the promotion of the growth of Chinese exports.

GVCs and China's iPhone exports

I start with the Phone, a popular high-technology good manufactured in a sophisticated value chain operated by Apple. In the iPhone value chain, Apple is in charge of the design and the iOS operating system, and outsources the production of iPhone parts and assembly to firms in Japan, Korea, China and elsewhere. All cross-border transactions associated with iPhone trade, such as the import of iPhone parts and the export of ready-to-use iPhones, are part of value chain trade. Until the time of writing, China had been the exclusive exporter of iPhones, including those sold in the US market. The fact that China exports iPhones to the US, where the iPhone was invented, appears inconsistent with both the Ricardian theory and Heckscher–Ohlin model, which predict that China should export low-skill, labor-intensive goods to the US, the leading nation in technology in the world. However, the fact that China exports iPhones to the US can be explained easily in terms of GVCs.

China's export of iPhones to the US and other countries is not a result of its technological superiority, but of its participation in Apple's value chain. On the back of each iPhone is the statement, "Designed by Apple in California Assembled in China." The message is clear: the role of China in the iPhone value chain is to assemble parts and components (most of which, particularly the core components, are made by other countries) into ready-to-use iPhones. As China is the iPhone assembly base, it is natural that iPhones available in the world market are shipped from China — to be counted as Chinese exports. However, a teardown analysis (Xing and Detert, 2010; Xing, 2020a) shows that no core components, including the CPU, NAND, DRAM and touch screen, were made by local Chinese firms. The technology required to make the iPhone is beyond the technological capacity of Chinese assembly firms. The phenomenon of exporting iPhones to the US and other foreign markets has nothing to do with China's indigenous technological capacity: it is mainly a result of the involvement of China in Apple's value chain. What China exports via the iPhone is the work of its low-skilled labor, embedded in the phone. It is the iPhone value chain that provides an opportunity for Chinese workers to sell their low-skilled services to the world's iPhone users. The rapid growth of Chinese iPhone exports cannot be attributed to any China-specific factors, but rather to the spillover effects of Apple's brand, advanced technology and online and offline Apple stores.

Figure 3.1 displays China's iPhone 2009 and 2015 exports to the US. In 2009, China exported 11.3 million iPhones valued at $2.02 billion to the US; in 2015 that figure jumped to 31.85 million

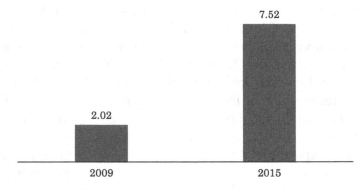

Figure 3.1   China's iPhone exports to the US (Billions US dollar)

Source: Xing and Detert (2010) and the author's estimates based on iPhone 6 teardown data from HIS, and iPhone Sales statistics from Finder.com.

units worth some $7.52 billion. In six years, China's iPhone exports to the US almost tripled in both volume and monetary value. To what extent was that dramatic increase related to China's technological advancement, comparative advantage in cheap labor, its dollar peg policy, or other China-specific factors? Virtually not at all.

First, between 2009 and 2015, the iPhone evolved from the iPhone 3G to the iPhone 6s, with an accompanying rise in retail price from $500 to $650. That increase in value of the iPhone suggests that the low price factor often associated with China's comparative advantage could not have been a contributing factor to the surge in Chinese iPhone exports to the US. As a matter of fact, from 2009 to 2015, the average nominal annual wage of Chinese workers rose from 32,700 yuan to 63,200 yuan, an increase of almost 100 percent. Not only that: during the same period the Chinese yuan appreciated against the US dollar by 8.8 percent, from 6.83 yuan/dollar to 6.23 yuan/dollar, so in fact the average wage of Chinese workers rose even more in the dollar terms than in the yuan. That wage increase and appreciation of the yuan indicate that the unit labor cost in China increased substantially, which in turn suggests that cheap labor and the so-called undervalued yuan could not be the reasons for the increase in the iPhone exports to the US. Therefore, the dramatic increase in the iPhone exports cannot be attributed to any China-specific factors; it is Apple's innovation and marketing activities that have increased American consumer demand for iPhones. More and more Americans have been attracted to the trendy design and cutting-edge technology of the iPhone, so Chinese factories assemble more iPhones and ship them to the US, hence driving the growth of Chinese iPhone exports to the US.

China's dominance of laptop computer exports is another example of GVC-driven export growth. Table 3.1 summarizes the explosive growth of the Chinese export of laptop computers during the period 2000–2018. In 2000, China exported 0.12 million units of laptop computers, valued at $210 million, less than one percent of world exports of laptop computers. By 2005, China's annual laptop computer exports jumped to 41.35 million units, more than half of the world exports. China exported laptops worth $29.9 billion,

Table 3.1   China's exports of laptop computers

Year	Value (Billion US dollar)	Percentage of the world laptop exports	Units (Million)	Percentage of the world laptop exports
2000	0.21	0.81	0.12	0.59
2005	29.90	53.4	41.35	55.9
2010	95.34	72.3	193.91	74.9
2018	95.88	70.3	250.20	70.3

Source: UNCOMTRADE and the author's calculations.

about 4 percent of total Chinese exports that year. That figure continued to surge, reaching 193.91 million units in 2010, accounting for three quarters of global laptop computer exports. In just a 10-year period, the export of Chinese laptop computers rose from less than one percent to 75 percent of world laptop exports. That change, arguably a miracle, intrigued Chinese watchers what magic had transformed China from a trivial player to the dominance in the world laptop market?

The laptop computer was invented by the Japanese company Toshiba. Laptop computers run on either the Windows operating system, owned by the American company Microsoft, or on Apple's operating system. Moreover, two American companies, Intel and AMD, have been monopolizing the market for CPUs, the heart of every personal computer. Clearly, China's technological capacity is not capable of the core technologies required to produce laptop computers. A teardown analysis of a HP laptop assembled in China reveals that no Chinese firm supplied any core components of the laptop, and the assembly by Chinese workers contributed a mere 6.1 percent of the total value added measured in the retail price (Dedrick *et al.*, 2010).

In 2017, Lenovo, the most popular Chinese laptop brand, had 20.2 percent of global laptop computer market; most of that came from sales in the Chinese market, not foreign markets. Lenovo was the only Chinese brand in the top 10 global brands of laptop computers. Outside the Chinese market, Lenovo's share was much smaller. Most of the Chinese made laptop computers in the global market are manufactured for foreign brands and the products of laptop value chains operated by foreign vendors. In 2017 HP was the largest laptop vendor, with 24.3 percent of the global market; Dell had 15.2 percent and Apple 9.6 percent (TrendForce, 2018). The world laptop computer market consists largely of competition among HP, Lenovo, DELL and Apple — it is not a scenario of competition between made in China laptop computers and those made elsewhere.

The modularization of personal computer production has enabled the development of value chains in the computer industry. Modules of computers can be designed independently and manufactured in geographically diverse locations. The rapid expansion of China's laptop computer sector is largely attributed to the relocation of assembly capacity from Taiwan to Mainland China. Before Mainland China emerged as the world largest exporter of personal computers, Taiwan was the major production base for ICT. To strengthen competitiveness and reduce production costs, Taiwanese firms gradually relocated their production to Mainland China in the 2000s, which dramatically boosted China's laptop computer production and export volume. By 2007, 97.5 percent of laptop computers made by Taiwan companies such as Foxconn, Pegatron and Compal Electronic, were manufactured in those firms' factories in Mainland China. The relocation of laptop value chains from Taiwan to Mainland China and the outsourcing of leading global PC vendors have transformed China into the world's leading laptop computer exporter (Xing, 2014).

GVCs and Chinese high-technology exports

iPhones and laptop computers are two distinctive products, both dependent on GVCs — but that may not be a sufficient basis for the argument that GVCs have been indispensable for the steady growth of China's exports. Here I expand the examination of Chinese exports to encompass all high-technology products, which account for about one-third of Chinese exports, and investigate the relationship between GVCs and China's high-technology export performance. As I discussed in Chapter 2, China has grown to become the leading high-technology exporting nation; its annual exports in this category have been consistently higher than those of the US, Germany and Japan. The US had a deficit in ATPs of more than $130 billion with China in 2018. Rodrik (2006) credited the Chinese government's science and technology policy for the remarkable performance of Chinese high-technology exports. Berger and Martin (2013) argued that China's dominance in a few high-tech products such as laptop computers and mobile phones could be attributed in part to the success of China's industrial policy.

It is true that China's R&D investment and industrial policy have contributed significantly to the enhancement of the technology capacity of Chinese industry. Nevertheless, it is difficult to imagine that those factors alone could drive China's high-technology exports to rise more than 600-fold in less than two decades, leaving even the US behind. Analysis of the manufacture of these high-technology exports and their sale in the global market indicate that China's remarkable success in high-technology exports was mainly attributable to its participation as an assembler in the GVCs of high-technology products — China was neither a technology leader nor a product inventor. Here I use the dependence of high-technology exports on processing exports as a quantitative measure of the linkage between GVCs and Chinese high-technology exports.

High-technology processing exports are made with imported parts, most of which are core technological components. Using imported components to make final goods (e.g., assembling iPhones) and exporting them abroad are value chain activities. Moreover, firms in China need to be certified by the Chinese customs to engage in processing trade, and they have to show contracts with foreign buyers when applying for processing trade status. In short, firms engaged in processing exports are contract manufacturers for foreign buyers, and they primarily assemble/manufacture for foreign MNCs, for example, iPhones for Apple, PS-4 game consoles for Sony and Kindles for Amazon. The binding contracts between Chinese processing firms and foreign buyers abroad, essential for the smooth operations of GVCs, define the relations between the two parties. Unambiguously, all high-technology

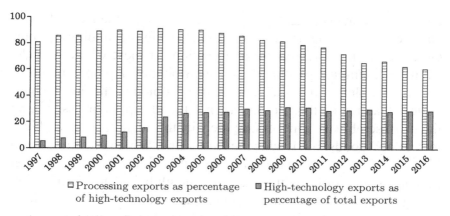

Figure 3.2 Dependence of China's high-technology exports on GVCs (Percentage)
Source: Calculated by the author based on Chinese Customs Office data.

processing exports are part of value chain trade. Processing export volume directly reflects the degree of GVC participation underlying Chinese high-technology exports.

Figure 3.2 shows the importance of processing exports in Chinese high-technology exports for the period 1997–2016. It also clarifies the share of high-technology goods in the overall exports of China during the period. The figure shows that, in 1997, 80.6 percent of Chinese high-technology exports were processing exports, i.e., more than 80 percent of Chinese high-technology exports were manufactured and exported along value chains. The intensity of value chain trade in high-technology exports had been increasing steadily: in 2003, more than nine-tenth of high-technology exports fell into the category of processing exports, further strengthening the dependence of Chinese high-technology exports on GVCs. Before the global financial crisis, processing exports consistently made up more than 80 percent of China's high-technology exports. This exceptionally high dependence on processing trade is unequivocal evidence that Chinese high-technology exporters have been deeply involved in high-technology GVCs. Chinese firms contributed value added to those products with their low-skilled labor services and standard peripheral parts; they did not contribute to the core technologies that determine the technological parameters and functionality of exported high-technology goods. Global consumer preferences and passion for these Chinese-made/Chinese-assembled products (e.g., smartphones, laptop computers, handheld tablets and digital cameras) are rooted in the new technological features of those products, not the cheap labor assembling them. Assembly is a necessary step in the manufacture of high-technology goods, but it adds the least value. Which country assembles these products generally has little impact on consumer purchasing decisions. China has been the global center of manufacturing and assembly, and Chinese-assembled high-technology exports have automatically grown with the technology innovation, increased brand popularity and expansion of the global distribution and retail networks of foreign MNCs.

For instance, HP, IBM, Dell, Cisco, Unisys, Microsoft and Intel were the top manufacturers of information technology for the US Federal government, but China was the overwhelming source of products for these manufacturers. On average, 51 percent of shipments to those seven commercial information technology manufacturers originated in China. Microsoft had the largest share of shipments originating in China, 73 percent (Beeny *et al.*, 2018). Unambiguously the value chains of those seven American manufacturers provided a conduit for Chinese made/assembled information technology to access the market of the US Federal government. Without participating in the value chains operated by the American companies, it would be impossible for Chinese made/assemble ICT to penetrate the market of the US Federal government at such a large scale. Again, China's emergence as the No. 1 high-tech exporting nation is mainly resulted from its participation in high-technology product value chains. The explosive growth of Chinese high-technology exports has primarily been driven by the foreign technologies embedded in the exports, by the foreign brands attached to those products, and by the foreign networks through which they have been distributed to and retailed on international markets.

In recent years, the appreciation of the yuan and the rising wages of Chinese workers have gradually eroded China's comparative advantage in the assembly of high-technology products. Some foreign MNCs have relocated their assembly facilities out of China, to countries such as Vietnam and India, where labor costs are even lower. Samsung, for instance, had completely shifted its Chinese smartphone assembly factories to Vietnam by 2019. In addition, Chinese firms have developed the technological capacity to produce substitutes for imported parts and components. The share of processing exports in China's high-technology exports has decreased steadily: by 2016, it had dropped to 60.8 percent, although it still accounted for more than half of total Chinese high-technology exports.

GVCs and China's overall exports

Not only had processing exports been a major export mode for Chinese high-technology goods but also for low-skilled and labor-intensive goods. Processing exports contributed most to the rapid growth of Chinese exports in the last 40 years. In the early 1980s, processing exports made up less than one-tenth of China's total exports. Supported by the favorable policy environment of that time, the growth of processing exports had constantly outpaced that of exports overall. The share of processing exports in China's total exports rose rapidly as Chinese exports became more and more dependent on GVCs. By 1995, processing exports accounted for 50 percent of Chinese exports, implying that at least a half of Chinese exports entered international markets via GVCs. Processing exports reached a peak of 57 percent in 1999. During the period 2000–2007, when Chinese exports were growing at more than 20 percent annually, processing exports consistently accounted for more than a half of Chinese exports. After the global financial crisis, that share gradually declined due to rising wages and the appreciation of the Chinese yuan. The slow growth of processing exports caused Chinese export growth to fall to less than 10 percent (Xing, 2018a). By 2018, processing exports accounted for only a third of China's total exports. The rise and fall of processing exports in the last four decades implies the decisive contribution of GVCs to the Chinese export miracle.

Analysis using processing exports as an indicator of GVC participation also shows that GVCs have functioned as an effective channel for the entry of Chinese goods into high-income countries. The US is the largest market for Chinese goods, Japan second. In general, the markets of high-income countries are more competitive than those of low-income nations. Consumers in high-income nations tend to be oriented toward brands and advanced technology, areas where Chinese firms generally have no comparative advantage. The proliferation of GVCs has offered an alternative path by which Chinese firms have penetrated the markets of high-income countries.

Processing exports were the dominant form of Chinese exports to the US, Japan and Germany, which attests to the importance of GVCs to the entry of made in China products into high-income countries. Figure 3.3 demonstrates the importance of processing trade in China's exports to the US, Japan and Germany from 1995 to 2014. In 1995, 69.2 percent of Chinese exports to the US were

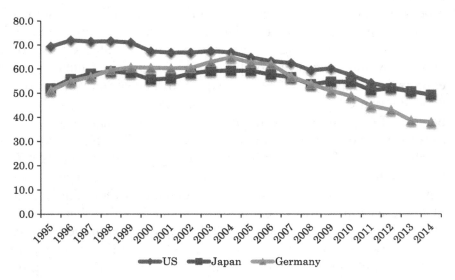

Figure 3.3   Share of processing exports in China's exports to the US, Japan and Germany (Percentage)

Source: The author's calculations, based on Chinese Customs Office data.

processing exports. In the following three years, the share of processing exports exceeded 70 percent each year. On average, processing exports comprised some 65 percent of China's exports to the US during the period 1995–2014. In the years leading up to 2005, Chinese processing exports to both Japan and Germany grew rapidly, much faster than ordinary exports — the share of Chinese processing exports to Japan rose from 52 percent in 1995 to 59 percent in 2005; in the same period, that of Germany increased from 51.2 percent to 65 percent. The overall share of processing exports gradually declined from that peak, although it was still about 50 percent for the US and Japan in 2014.

Walmart and Chinese exports to the US

For Chinese firms striving to sell products to global consumers, processing exports are one means of entry into the global market. In the case of low cost and labor-intensive products such as apparel, shoes, toys, furniture and accessories, which Chinese firms can produce with entirely domestic inputs, thousands of Chinese firms have participated as designated suppliers in buyer-driven value chains typically led by large retailers such as Walmart, Kmart, Costco, The Home Depot and Target. In the last few decades, large retailers have participated to a greater and greater extent in international markets and have become a driving force of international trade. They have sourced directly from foreign manufacturers and bypassed distributors. In addition, large retailers specify product designs, set product standards, help manufacturers promote their products, and provide suppliers with information about consumer behaviors and tastes (Nordas, 2008). Large retailers have garnered a larger and larger share of overall retail: in the US, large retailers represented 9 percent of all US imports and 60 percent of the total value of imports from China (Bernard *et al.*, 2010). In terms of the bilateral trade with China, large US retailers are much more active than smaller ones. It was estimated that large US retailers' marginal propensity to import from China was 17 percentage points higher than that of smaller ones (Basker and Pham, 2007). The expansion of retail chains has brought imports to more locations and has reduced retailers' marginal costs, prompting further expansion of the market for imports. At the same time, interaction between chain size and import volume has amplified the growth of imports.

Walmart is the largest retailer in the US. By 2018, it had more than 4,500 stores, located in all 50 states, along with more than 550 Sam's Clubs. Walmart accounted for 6.5 percent of all US retail sales, and by the end of 2005, 46 percent of Americans lived within five miles of a Walmart or a Sam's Club Store, and 88 percent lived within 15 miles of one or the other (Basker and Pham, 2007). "Everyday low prices" is the motto of Walmart stores: Walmart specializes in relatively low-end products whose production does not require large human or physical investment. The emergence of China as a center of low-cost production enabled the formation of the Walmart China joint venture, a catalyst for rising US imports from China. More than 80 percent of Walmart's 60,000 suppliers were in China; Walmart's global procurement office was located in Shenzhen, China (Gereffi and Christian, 2009). All Chinese suppliers of Walmart belong to its value chains. Their products are sold to American consumers via Walmart's retail networks, a necessary infrastructure for accessing American households. The division of labor between the Chinese suppliers and Walmart frees the Chinese suppliers from the necessity of fixed investment in marketing, distribution and retail networks — and the Chinese suppliers do not need an understanding of the preferences of American consumers, or trends in consumer goods. Following the instructions of Walmart on product designs and standards, these Chinese firms produce goods and ship them to the US, where they become Chinese exports to the US.

Figure 3.4 displays the astonishing growth of Walmart imports from China during the period 2001–2013. In 2001, Walmart imported $9.5 billion in Chinese goods; five years later that figure almost tripled to $26.7 billion. By 2013, Walmart imports from China had increased almost five-fold, surging to $49.1 billion, equivalent to almost 10 percent of the US imports from China that year. Besides the low cost advantage of the Chinese goods, the rapid expansion of the Walmart chain in the US was a critical factor

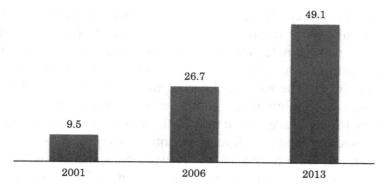

Figure 3.4　Walmart imports from China (Billion US dollar)
Source: Scott (2015).

driving the explosive growth of Walmart imports from China. If these Chinese firms had not been designated Walmart suppliers, their exports to the US would not have been able to jump five-fold in such a short period, nor could these Chinese suppliers have tapped the US retail networks to the extent that they did.

Like Walmart, many global fashion brand vendors have most of their contract suppliers located in China. In 2018, UNIQLO had more than 90 percent of its suppliers in China, H&M had more than 800 Chinese suppliers and Nike had more than 100. These factoryless manufacturers concentrate on product design, distribution and retailing, while their Chinese suppliers specialize in production. At the outset, it was low production costs in China that attracted brand vendors to source their products from China; later it is the brand vendors' fashionable designs and the expansion of global chains that have driven the worldwide growth of exports of made in China products.

Measuring China's GVC participation: Processing exports vs. the GVC participation index

There is not a universally agreed measure of GVC participation. In this chapter, I primarily employ the share of processing exports to quantify the linkage between GVCs and Chinese exports, and to analyze the extent to which participation in GVCs contributed to China's export miracle. The OECD proposed a GVC participation index, a sum of a backward participation index and a forward participation index. The backward participation index is defined as the percentage of foreign value added in a country's gross exports, while the forward index is the ratio of the domestic value added used as intermediate inputs of foreign countries' exports to a country's gross exports. Both backward and forward participation indices are estimated by using international input–output tables. However, the highly aggregated sector classification of international input–output tables cannot map the critical relations among firms participating in value chains. As Kaplinsky (2013) commented, "the sector classification used in even the most disaggregated input-output tables is too blunt to capture the sorts of flows evidenced in the detailed analysis of the iPhone." In addition, the assumptions made in the construction of national input–output tables, such as the proportionality of imported inputs across all sectors, oversimplify the micro-features of GVCs and undermine reliability. When input–output tables for various countries are linked across borders, these problems are compounded and statisticians may have to "cook the books" in order to achieve consistency among input–output tables from multiple countries (Sturgeon *et al.*, 2013). Last but not least, the GVC participation index focuses only on the production stages of value chains, and fails to capture the linkage of GVCs beyond production stages. Chinese exports, which are final goods with zero foreign value added, but are manufactured for foreign brand vendors or large retailers, are part of value chain trade. For instance, Chinese-made UNIQLO jeans sold in overseas markets and Chinese goods made for Walmart stores in the US all belong to value chain trade, but they represent a different means of GVC participation. According to the definition of the GVC participation index, this group of Chinese exports is not treated as part of GVC-related exports — which understates the reliance of Chinese exports on GCVs.

Figure 3.5 compares two quantitative measures of China's GVC participation during the period 2005–2015. For each year, the left

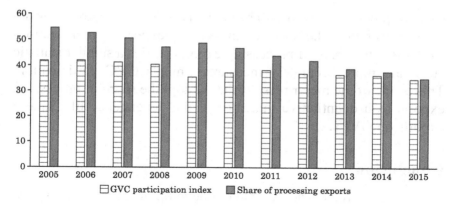

Figure 3.5 Measures of China's GVC participation: Share of processing exports vs. the GVC participation index (Percentage)

Source: The author's calculations and OECD TiVA database.

bar represents the GVC participation index, the sum of the backward and forward indices retrieved from OECD TiVA database; the right bar shows the share of processing exports (adopted in this book as a measure of the lower boundary of China's GVC participation). The disparity between the two measures is significant. In general, the GVC participation index proposed by OECD substantially underestimate the level of China's GVC participation. Each year between 2005 and 2010, the GVC participation index was more than 10 percentage points lower than the share of processing exports. In particular, the GVC participation index for 2005 was 41.9 percent but the share of processing exports was 54.7 percent, 12.8 percentage points higher than the GVC participation index. For 2010, even though the gap between the two measures had fallen to 9.6 percentage points, the GVC participation index still substantially underestimates China's GVC participation. The two measures did gradually converge: in 2015, the GVC participation index was 0.3 percentage points lower than the share of processing exports. As explained before, the share of processing exports measures the lower boundary of China's GVC participation. The actual level of its GVC participation should be higher than that indicated by the share of processing exports. The GVC participation index is consistently lower than the share of processing exports, which demonstrates that the share of processing exports carries a smaller statistic error and more accurately measures China's GVC participation. This is one of the major reasons that I adopt the share of processing exports as a quantitative indicator of the dependence of Chinese exports on GVCs.

Conclusion

In less than three decades, China, a developing country, surpassed the US, Japan and Germany in exports, and emerged as the leading exporting nation in the world. This significant achievement has been referred to as a miracle. Many theories have been proposed to account for China's emergence as the largest trading nation, and for the popularity and competitiveness of Chinese goods worldwide. To date, studies of the phenomenon generally point to China's open door policy, comparative advantage in labor-intensive products, exchange rate regime, accession to the WTO, and domestic institutional reforms — and to inflows of foreign direct investment (FDI).

This chapter examines China's growth from a completely new perspective, arguing that it is China's integration into GVCs that played a crucial role in fostering China's transformation into an export miracle. This GVC perspective can explain China's trade profile as the largest high-technology exporter in the world despite its developing country status, and as the sole exporter of the iPhone to the US, a seeming contradiction to the classic comparative advantage theory. The emergence of GVCs as a main production model has revolutionized the organization of international trade. We now see a new division of labor where Chinese exporters have specialized in production tasks and GVC lead firms are responsible for research and development, product design, brand promotion, production distribution and retailing. That division of labor has freed Chinese firms from the need for fixed investment, and helped them overcome barriers to entry into international markets. It is no longer true that only large, productive firms with economies of scale can successfully engage in exporting. Fixed investment in marketing research, brand promotion and the building of infrastructure, previously essential for selling products globally in traditional international trade, are no longer necessary for Chinese exporters who have participated in GVCs.

I identify three generators of GVC spillover effects: brands; technology and product innovations; distribution and retailing networks. Chinese firms participating in the GVCs of various manufactured products have benefited tremendously from those spillover effects. The internationally recognized brand logos that appear on made in China products have not only lowered entry barriers for Chinese products but also strengthened their competitiveness and global popularity. The technology and product innovations of GVC lead firms have given rise to new markets and boosted consumer demand, which in turn increased demand not only for Chinese assembly services but also for parts and components supplied by Chinese firms, thus driving the growth of Chinese exports. By participating in GVCs, Chinese firms are able to have all their products sold via global distribution and retail networks, which have greatly enhanced the access of Chinese goods to global consumers.

China's iPhone trade and its dominance of the laptop computer sector are a result of GVC participation, not China's comparative advantage in technology. Processing exports are synonymous with value chain trade. The use of imported materials to make exports is a typical GVC activity; it is a direct measure of the participation of Chinese firms in value chains. Using processing exports to measure China's participation in GVCs is more intuitive and accurate than the GVC participation index proposed by the OECD. The extraordinarily high share of processing exports in Chinese high-technology exports makes it very clear that the emergence of China as the topmost high-tech exporting nation is attributed mainly to China's role as a global center for assembly of high-technology products, and not to China's science and technology policy or intrinsic comparative advantage.

Processing exports are a subset of GVC activities. They had been a major export mode for Chinese goods to enter international markets and contributed significantly to the Chinese export miracle. In bilateral trade, processing exports enabled made in China products to smoothly enter the markets of high-income nations. Besides Chinese firms in processing exports, those in low-value and labor-intensive consumer sectors such as apparel, shoes, toys and accessories have entered buyer-driven value chains as designated suppliers. They have manufactured final products for foreign buyers without using imported intermediates, and their products, carrying foreign brands, have been distributed globally via retail outlets operated by those buyers. The worldwide expansion of retail chains such as Walmart, has led to a steady increase in demand for Chinese goods. That alliance between Walmart and Chinese suppliers is a clear demonstration of how GVCs have been a key driver of China's export miracle.

Chapter 4

The China–US Trade Imbalance from the GVC Perspective

The US trade deficit with China has increased tremendously since China entered the World Trade Organization (WTO). In 2018, China accounted for almost half of the $875 billion US trade deficit in goods with the entire world; back in 2001, the year China was officially admitted as a member of the WTO, it contributed less than 20 percent to the overall US trade deficit. The persistently huge US trade deficit triggered a protracted trade war between the two largest economies in the world. In its multiple-round trade negotiations with China, the Trump administration repeatedly demanded that China should massively increase the purchase of American products so as to reduce the trade deficit. As a result, in the phase one trade agreement signed by President Trump and Chinese Vice Premier Liu He in Washington DC on January 15, 2020, the Chinese government committed to raising its purchases of American goods and services by $200 billion by the end of 2021. If that target could be achieved, China's imports of American goods and services would be more than double to those in 2017, and would dramatically reduce the US trade deficit.

For searching the roots of the trade imbalance between China and the US, mainstream economists tend to emphasize the low savings rate of American households. They claim that American households have a very low savings rate because they prefer consumption to saving, and even worse, they often spend beyond their means, as evidenced by the sustained high individual debts in the US. The excessive propensity of American households to consume has been a critical driver of the robust demand for imports, and the steadily rising trade deficit is simply a natural result of that kind of reckless consumption (Frankel, 2009; Yu, 2018). This argument is supported by the savings–investment relation derived from the standard gross domestic product (GDP) identity, which suggests that in an open economy, a country's trade deficit always mirrors its net external borrowing. China, Japan and many oil exporting nations in the Middle East have purchased large quantities of US government bonds, effectively lending their domestic savings to the US. Looking at the other side of the savings–investment equation, former US Federal Reserve Chairman Bernanke (2005) argued that the savings glut (excess savings accumulated in those foreign countries) is responsible for the persistent and massive US trade deficit.

Trade balance is defined as the difference between exports and imports. The arguments surrounding low savings rates and savings glut typically emphasize the role of import demand in trade imbalances. While an increase in imports due to robust domestic demand can inherently worsen a trade deficit, a decrease in exports can lead to a similar result. Instead of focusing on American consumers' demand for foreign goods, President Trump emphasized that restrictions on American exports to China shaped the bilateral trade imbalance. He blamed unfair Chinese government trade practices and the non-reciprocal tariff structure between the two nations for the massive trade deficit. He frequently complained that the Chinese government imposes relatively high tariffs so as to restrict the access of American goods to the Chinese market (White House, 2018). For example, China levied a 25 percent tariff on American automobiles before the trade war started, while at the same time the US imposed a mere 2.5 percent on Chinese automobile imports. Because of the trade war, the Chinese government voluntarily lowered its automobile tariff to 15 percent in July 2018, a friendly gesture in response to the US complaints, though that rate is still multiples of the counterpart 2.5 percent. According to the World Bank (2018), in 2018 the average Chinese tariff on all tradable goods was 10 percent, while that of the US was 2.74 percent. This asymmetric tariff structure implies that the US market was more open to foreign goods than the Chinese market. Doubtless, Chinese trade barriers effectively have hindered American exports to the Chinese market, indirectly increasing the US trade deficit with China — which is why President Trump had been striving to achieve fair and reciprocal trade with China and insisting on leveling the playing field in trade with China.

Some Chinese economists (e.g., Ren, 2018; Li, 2019) insist that the dominance of the US dollar in the global economy is at base the result of the US trade deficit with China, since the US has to channel sufficient dollar liquidity through trade deficits to support the international financial system, which is centered on the US dollar. Since the collapse of the Bretton Woods system, the US dollar has been the dominant currency for international trade and investment settlements. The theoretical foundation of that argument is the "Triffin dilemma," an argument used to critique the Bretton Woods System, under which the US dollar was designated as the only currency for international transactions, and all other countries pegged their currencies to the US dollar, backed by gold at the fixed price of $35 per ounce of gold. Under that arrangement, the US was obliged to supply sufficient dollar liquidity to the world economy — but then it would be inevitable for the US to have a current account deficit — or if the US eliminated its balance of payments deficit, it would deprive global trade of international liquidity (Bordo and McCauley, 2017).

Using the Triffin dilemma to interpret the trade imbalance between China and the US is based on a fundamentally flawed argument. In the post Bretton Woods era, the Triffin dilemma no longer exists. In 1971, President Nixon abandoned the Bretton Woods System and unilaterally cancelled the convertibility of the US dollar to gold. Since then, the world economy has moved into a regime of free-floating exchange rates. Now other currencies besides the US dollar can be used for the conduct of international trade. The British pound, the Japanese yen, the Swiss franc, and now the euro are all used in international transactions. The conduct of world trade and investment activities is generally not confined by the liquidity constraint of the US dollar. Even if the Triffin dilemma were a reasonable argument, there would be no economic rationale to justify the flight to China of almost half of the necessary dollar liquidity supplied through the US trade deficit.

America's low savings rate, China's trade barriers and the dollar's dominance may all be factors contributing to the trade imbalance, and may partially explain why the US has been running a huge trade deficit with China. On the other hand, the explosive growth of the deficit after China's entry into the WTO suggests that those factors are far from sufficient to account for the soaring deficit. There must be structural variables driving the exceptional expansion of the US trade deficit with China.

Figure 4.1 presents the US trade deficit with China in 2001 and 2018, along with the overall trade deficit of the US and its trade deficit with Japan, for reference. In 2001, the US trade deficit with China amounted to $83.1 billion, about 19.2 percent of the total US trade deficit. Seventeen years later, in 2018, the deficit increased more than five-fold, jumping to $419.5 billion. In contrast, in the interval between 2001 and 2018, the total US trade deficit grew at

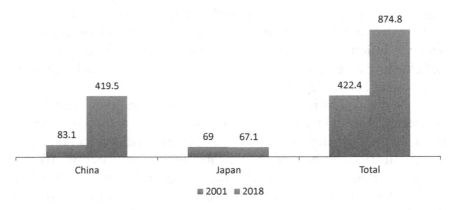

Figure 4.1   US trade deficit with China and Japan, 2001 and 2018 (Billions US dollar)

Source: US Census Bureau.

a much slower pace, increasing to $874.8 billion, slightly more than double that in 2001. Consequently, the cross-country distribution of the US trade deficit skewed startlingly toward China, with virtually half coming from China. The low rate of savings by American households, a factor determining US demand for imports, cannot fully account for the concentration of the US trade deficit in one country, rather than proportional distribution across all trading partners.

During the period 2001–2018, US GDP doubled, rising from $10 trillion to $20.5 trillion. The US trade deficit to GDP ratio changed little; it was 4 percent in 2001 and rose to just 4.3 percent in 2018, i.e., the growth of the US trade deficit was in line with that of its income, and the consumption behavior of American consumers, especially their preference for foreign goods, did not change at all. If the low savings rate were one of the major factors determining the bilateral trade deficit, the US trade deficit with China would have risen in proportion to its GDP, rather than quadrupling.

Figure 4.1 also provides an outline of the history of the trade balance between the US and Japan, the second largest source of the US trade deficit. In contrast to the dramatic increase in the deficit with China, the deficit with Japan fell slightly, from $69.0 billion to $67.1 billion, in the interval 2001–2018. If the low savings rate and American consumers' passion for foreign goods drove the deficit with China to surge more than four-fold, why would not those forces also expand the deficit with Japan? Japanese automobiles, game consoles, digital cameras and many other electronic products remain popular with American households. It would be unimaginable that, with their income doubling over that period, American consumers only increased their expenditures on made in China products, and not on Japanese products.

The low savings rate and the Triffin dilemma simply ascribe the US trade imbalance to excessive demand by American households, while the unfair trade argument emphasizes obstacles undermining American firms' access to the Chinese market. In effect, the proponents of these arguments ignore the role of global value chains (GVCs) in facilitating the penetration of Chinese exports into the

US market and the growth of the bilateral trade imbalance. As explained in Chapter 3, most Chinese goods enter the US market via GVCs led by multinational corporations (MNCs), including American MNCs. Chinese exports manufactured along GVCs consist of not only domestically made intermediates but also foreign made parts and components. They embody a large portion of foreign value added. This is a distinguishing feature of Chinese exports to the US. Using conventional trade statistics to measure and interpret bilateral trade balances is misleading; it seriously distorts the magnitude of bilateral trade balances and the status of bilateral payments.

Conventional trade statistics are compiled with an implicit assumption that the whole gross value of exports is created by the exporting nation. This assumption is not valid for value chain trade. The inconsistency between value chain trade realities and current trade statistics gives rise to a distortion of bilateral trade imbalances. In recent decades, China has served as an assembly center for various manufactured products sold in the US market. Conventional trade statistics implicitly assume that the whole value added of Chinese exports is originated in China, regardless of whether foreign intermediates are used in the exports or not; this greatly exaggerates China's export volume as well as its trade surplus with the US. For value chain trade, conventional trade statistics are not reliable for the assessment of bilateral trade balances.

Meanwhile, as China has been evolving into a global manufacturing center, many American MNCs have evolved into factoryless manufacturers by outsourcing all production tasks to foreign companies and concentrating only on non-production tasks. American factoryless manufacturers have no production facilities, but they retain the ownership of their products assembled or manufactured by contract manufacturers. The global operations of American factoryless manufacturers have brought about a geographic separation of product manufacturing and ownership, which challenges the applicability of current trade statistics system to value chain-based modern trade. Even though American factoryless manufacturers export to China billion dollars in services and value added of their intellectual property embedded in physical products assembled by foreign contract manufacturing, trade statistics do not record those export activities and thus greatly underestimate the volume of US exports to China. This failure is also due in part to the disconnect between value chain trade and the now outdated system for calculation of trade volumes. In terms of income generation, the export of the value added of the intellectual property and services embedded in physical products has the same function as the export of physical goods such as grain or cars. This new type of exports emerges along value chains, but current trade statistics practice cannot measure and record this type of exports. China is the largest overseas market for the products of a few factoryless American MNCs including Apple, Nike, Qualcomm and AMD. As a result, current trade statistics effectively underestimate US exports to China — another important reason why the US trade deficit with China expanded rapidly in the last decades.

How the US trade deficit with China is exaggerated

Economists prefer to study large samples in empirical studies. They tend to dismiss case analyses as focused on biased outliers of a population. However, a representative case analysis can be intuitively valid, convincing and powerful, for rejecting conventional narratives or norms. The case of the iPhone is a strong intuitive demonstration of (a) the unsuitability of conventional trade statistics for evaluation of value chain trade, and (b) the extent to which those statistics exaggerate China's exports to, and trade surplus with, the US.

iPhones are designed and marketed by Apple, one of the most innovative American companies. They are manufactured and retailed via a sophisticated value chain. Apart from software and product design, most of the production of iPhones takes place outside the US. Apple restricts the sales of iPhones to Apple stores, online shops and direct sales agreements with service providers worldwide.

Manufacturing of the first generation iPhone, the iPhone 3G, involved nine companies, located in China, Korea, Japan, Germany and the US. The major producers and suppliers of the iPhone parts and components included Toshiba, Samsung, Infineon, Broadcom, Numonyx, Murata, Dialog Semiconductor and Cirrius Logic. All iPhone 3G components produced by these companies were shipped to Foxconn's factories in Shenzhen, China for assembly into final products, and then exported to the US and the rest of the world. The process of manufacturing the iPhone 3G reveals how GVCs function in international trade; why a developing country such as China can export (at least according to the currently applied methodology for calculating trade statistics) a state of the art high-technology good; and how the US, the country that invented the iPhone, becomes an importer of it.

Table 4.1 shows the costs and major suppliers of iPhone 3G components and parts. Japanese company Toshiba supplied the flash memory, display module and touch screen; Korea's Samsung manufactured the application processor and the SDRAM-Mobile DDR; the baseband, the camera module RF transceiver and the GPS were sourced from Germany's Infineon. Virtually all major components were supplied by non-Chinese companies. The bill of materials for the iPhone 3G totaled $178.96, the production cost of the phone. Within the iPhone value chain, Chinese labor performed the least value added iPhone production task, earning $6.50 for assembly of each iPhone 3G, a mere 3.6 percent of the production cost. The teardown data in Table 4.1 indicate that the technology embedded in the iPhone 3G, which determines the functions of the phone, has nothing to do with China.

Since all iPhones are assembled entirely in China, current trade statistics rules record ready-to-use iPhones shipped from China to the US as an export of China to the US, making them part of the US trade deficit. When Foxconn shipped one iPhone 3G to the US, it declared an export value of $178.96 because it is a contract manufacturer of Apple and does not own the iPhone. Therefore, whenever an iPhone 3G was shipped to foreign markets, this $178.96 was recorded as a Chinese export. In 2009, China shipped 11.3 million iPhones to the US. Accordingly, China's iPhone exports to the US amounted some $2 billion. For its assembly of all iPhones that year,

Table 4.1   Bill of materials of the iPhone 3G

Manufacturer	Component	Cost (US dollar)
Toshiba (Japan)	Flash memory	24.00
	Display module	19.25
	Touch screen	16.00
Samsung (Korea)	Application processor	14.46
	SDRAM-Mobile DDR	8.50
Infineon (Germany)	Baseband	13.00
	Camera module	9.55
	RF transceiver	2.80
	GPS receiver	2.25
	Power IC RF function	1.25
Broadcom (USA)	Bluetooth/FM/WLAN	5.95
Numonyx (USA)	Memory MCP	3.65
Murata (Japan)	FEM	1.35
Dialog Semiconductor (Germany)	Power IC application processor function	1.30
Cirrus Logic (USA)	Audio codec	1.15
Other bill of materials		*48.00*
Total bill of materials		*172.46*
Manufacturing cost		*6.50*
Grand total		*178.96*

Source: Xing and Detert (2010).

China imported $121.5 million in parts from the US, all made by American companies Broadcom, Numonyx and Cirrus Logic. Subtracting the value of imported parts from the US from the total export value of $2 billion yields $1.9 billion, China's calculated trade surplus resulting from the iPhone trade. From the perspective of the US, that $1.9 billion was an American trade deficit. This is how current trade statistics methods calculate exports and trade balance related to the iPhone trade.

As displayed in Table 4.1, most of the export value and the US deficit associated with the iPhone were actually attributed to parts and components imported from third countries such as Japan, Korea and Germany, and had nothing to do with China. Chinese workers simply assembled those parts and components, contributing only $6.50 in value added for each iPhone 3G. However, the conventional method for measuring trade assumes that all of the $178.96 in parts in an iPhone 3G shipped to the US were created by China, incorrectly crediting it to China, a substantial exaggeration of both China's export volume and its trade surplus. For assessing China's contribution to the iPhone trade and the corresponding trade deficit between China and the US, China's value added rather than the gross value should be used.

Table 4.2 shows China's trade with the US in the iPhone 3G and the corresponding balances measured in both gross value and value added. A breakdown of the value added across the countries involved in manufacturing the iPhone suggests that, of the $1.9 billion trade surplus resulting from the export of those iPhones, only $73 million, or about 3.8 percent, originated in China, with the rest coming from Germany, Japan, Korea and other non-US countries. Similarly, in terms of Chinese value added, China's iPhone export would be $73 million, a tiny fraction of that calculated using gross value methodology. The significant difference between the two calculation methods demonstrates that conventional trade statistics greatly exaggerate China's iPhone exports and the related trade surplus. Counting the value added of intermediates from foreign countries either as part of Chinese exports or as a trade surplus does not make economic sense, especially when economists and policy makers are searching for ways of reducing the trade imbalance.

Table 4.2   China's iPhone 3G exports to the US in 2009

Total shipment	11.3 million unit
Unit price	$178.96
Gross value	$2 billion
Trade surplus in gross value	$1.9 billion
Trade surplus in value added	$73 million

Source: Xing and Detert (2010).

It is important to emphasize that using value added to calculate China's exports to and trade balance with the US is not just an academic exercise. It is critical for economists and policy makers to correctly evaluate the balance of payments implications of value chain trade. Generally national governments regard trade deficits as an economic problem because it represents net income outflows resulting from international trade. In the age of the gold standard, a trade deficit was seen as a loss of gold reserve. Even two centuries ago, economists proved that free trade is mutually welfare enhancing and better than autarky. In the 21st century, the world economy remains far from a free trade configuration. All governments still prefer exports to imports and strive to have a trade surplus, a net income inflow from foreign countries. For value chain trade, it is the lead firms of GVCs, not the contract manufacturers assembling final products, who pay suppliers directly for all sourced intermediates and services. In other words, all parts used in the iPhone are purchased by Apple directly from the suppliers, and the income associated with the purchase goes to the countries where the parts are made, not China. In the case of the iPhone trade, if China exported one iPhone 3G, only $6.50 in income flew to China as a payment for the assembly service, despite the fact that the Chinese export to the US was recorded as $178.96. Similarly, trade statistics show that 2009 exports of the iPhone from China to the US totaled $2 billion, although there was no corresponding $2 billion income transfer from the US to China. As a matter of fact, only $73 million, the payment for assembly, went to China for the total shipment of 11.3 million iPhones to the US. Therefore, value added in trade is a measure of both actual contribution of exports to an economy and actual income flows associated with value chain trade.

In 2018, Apple launched the iPhone X, the first smartphone with a price tag of over $1,000. The steady rise of the price of the iPhone has not dampened the phone's popularity and the strong demand for it. However, even now, as the iPhone has evolved beyond 12th generation, trade statistics are still analyzed in a stone-age fashion, which means that the statistical distortion of bilateral trade figures is more pronounced than ever.

More Chinese companies participated in iPhone X value chain than participated in iPhone 3G value chain, and those participating in iPhone X value chain performed relatively sophisticated tasks, well beyond simply assembly. Together, they contributed $104 in value added to each iPhone X, about 25.4 percent of the total $409.24 production cost of the iPhone X, which implies that for every iPhone X sold in the global market, China receives $104 (Xing, 2020a). The value added captured by Chinese firms for each assembled iPhone X is dramatically higher than that for each first generation iPhone. Figure 4.2 shows the cross country distribution of the production cost of the iPhone X. Specifically, of the $409.25 total bill of materials for the iPhone X, the US contributed 18.7 percent, Korea 25.8 percent and Japan 19.3 percent. Korea contributed most to the production of the iPhone X, followed by China, Japan and the US. Despite the impressive increase in value added captured by the Chinese firms, all core components were still supplied by American, Japanese and Korean companies.

Similar to the case of the iPhone 3G, when China ships one iPhone X to the US, the current system of trade statistics calculates it as a $409.25 export to the US. By subtracting the $76.50 value of the parts imported from the US, it is straightforward to find that the import of an iPhone X results in a $332.75 trade deficit for the US. As can be seen in Figure 4.2, Korea, Japan and other non-US countries are also involved in the production of the iPhone, supplying

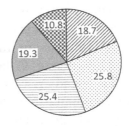

US   Korea   China   Japan   Other

Figure 4.2 Distribution of the iPhone X value added by country (Production only, Percentage)

Source: Xing (2020a).

more than 45 percent of the parts and components — so using $332.75 as a proxy for the US iPhone trade deficit with China is clearly an exaggeration of the bilateral trade balance; that figure actually reflects the trade deficit between the US and the other countries involved in the value chain. If measured in value added, the US deficit with China for the import of one iPhone X is only $104, less than one-third of the figure based on gross value. The difference between the two estimates is $228.75, implying that for every iPhone X imported, current trade statistics mistakenly add $228.75 to the US trade deficit with China.

It is estimated that in 2017 American consumers bought 42.2 million units of iPhones (Finder, 2019), all of them imported from China. Using this figure as a reference, I estimated that the iPhone trade inflated the US trade deficit with China in 2018 by $9.65 billion, about 2.3 percent of the total US deficit with China. In 2009, the statistical distortion related to the export of the iPhone 3G was estimated at $1.83 billion, less than 0.8 percent of the US trade deficit with China. Therefore, iPhone trade remains a significant source of statistical distortion in calculations of the China–US bilateral trade imbalance. The statistical distortion is much greater than before, given the success of Apple products and the ongoing use of outdated trade statistics methodology.

The two cases of iPhone models convincingly demonstrate that conventional trade statistics significantly inflate China's trade imbalance with the US. Clearly value added is a better tool than gross value of trade for the evaluation of bilateral trade balances and payments. The iPhone is a unique and successful product, but it is not an outlier among thousands of Chinese exports to the US, since most of those exports are manufactured in the same fashion. Statistical distortion of the bilateral trade balance between China and the US is not confined to iPhone trade. Exports of any made in China product containing imported foreign inputs are subject to similar distortion. WTO and IDE-JETRO (2011) used inter-regional input–output tables to estimate the aggregated distortion of the bilateral trade balance between China and the US. Their joint study found that China's trade surplus with the US in terms of gross trade value is 10 percent higher than that measured in value added.

Johnson and Noguera (2012) also used the input–output table approach to calculate the value added content of China–US trade. They showed that the 2004 US–China trade imbalance would be 30–40 percent smaller if it were measured in value added. To gauge the distortion of the total bilateral trade balance, I resorted to UIBE-GVC Indicators, which provide by-country estimates of domestic value added for large commodity groups and total exports. I found that in 2015 China's overall trade surplus with the US, calculated as value added, was 56 percent of that surplus calculated as gross value, and the trade surplus measured in value added for computers, electronics and optical, the largest product category, was 41 percent of that calculated as gross value (Figure 4.3). Clearly, if the value added approached were adopted, and I think it should be, the bilateral trade imbalance between China and the US would be halved. For evaluation of bilateral trade balances, the adoption of the value added approach is essential when value chain trade becomes a mainstream mode of production. The value added approach would not only reduce trade friction but more importantly also enable economists and policy makers to

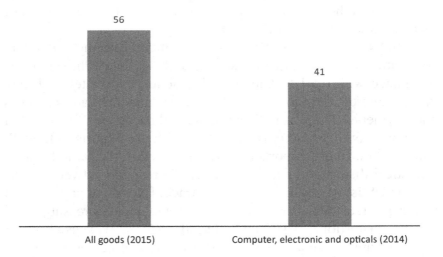

Figure 4.3   US trade deficit with China in value added (Deficit in gross value = 100)

Source: The author's calculation based on UIBE-GVC Indexes and World Bank (2019).

correctly assess the status of bilateral payments associated with international trade.

How US exports to China are underestimated: Apple's "missing exports"

At present, there is a consensus among economists and international organizations, including the WTO, the IMF and the World Bank, that value added in trade is a better measure than gross value for assessing bilateral trade balances. TiVA, compiled by the Organisation for Economic Co-operation and Development (OECD), has become a more and more popular tool for the study of trade issues. On the other hand, the exaggeration of China's exports to and trade surplus with the US is just one of the two sources of the distortion on the bilateral trade balance between the two countries. The other source is the fact that current trade statistics actually underestimate the US exports to China and the rest of the world, contributing to the distortion of the bilateral trade balance too.

Many American MNCs have adopted GVC strategy. They now concentrate primarily on brand marketing, product design and technological innovation, and generally outsource manufacturing and assembly tasks to foreign companies. This emergent international division of labor along GVCs has transformed these American MNCs into factoryless manufacturers, which do not produce any physical products but sell foreign consumers the value added of their services and intangible assets embedded in goods assembled/ produced by external contract manufacturers. Deriving revenues in international markets from the services and intangible assets embedded in physical products constitutes a new type of international trade inherent in GVCs. This kind of trade differs intrinsically from conventional service trade, as factoryless MNCs do not license their brands, technology or other type of intellectual property to third parties for royalties or fees. Factoryless American MNCs generally capture the largest share of the value added of their products sold in international markets, thanks to their monopolistic power over intellectual property such as brands and patented technologies.

Generally trade statistics, including exports, imports and trade balances, are calculated based on the value of goods crossing national borders. If goods are shipped from a country, across one of its borders and declared at its customs, the shipment is recorded as an export from that country, i.e., the physical crossing of a national border is a necessary criterion for including the value of shipped goods in trade statistics. Current trade statistics, however, fail to record the earnings of American factoryless manufacturers from outsourced production abroad as an export of the US, because (1) the products sold to foreign consumers do not cross the US borders, and (2) the value added of intellectual property and services are embedded in physical products, not sold separately as the case for royalties and license fees. In this light, current statistics greatly underestimate US exports.

The case of the iPhone X is pertinent here. A Chinese consumer buying an iPhone X pays $1,000 to Apple, of which $409.25 is payment for the parts and assembly service, and the remaining $590.75 is essentially a payment for the provision of the design, the iOS operating system, marketing activities, and the strong brand name. This $590.75 actually reflects a sale of Apple's services, provided by Apple employees working at the headquarters in California. The transaction, however, is not classified as a US export to China, because the iPhone X enters the Chinese market directly from the assembly plant in China; no iPhone X sold in China crosses the US borders. In the aforementioned analysis, for simplicity, I assume that no post-production services are provided by Chinese workers. For perfectly accurate calculation of the actual value added contributed by Apple to the iPhone X, it is necessary to exclude the value added of related retail services rendered by Chinese workers.

Chinese consumers' passion for trendy Apple products has turned China into Apple's largest foreign market. In 2015, Apple's sales in China amounted to $56.5 billion, which exceeded sales of soybeans, airplanes and every other single good imported by

China from the US. In short, Apple captures the largest share of the value added of Apple products purchased by Chinese consumers. According to Apple's Form 10-K for that year, the average gross margin of all Apple products was 40 percent. It was estimated that, of the $56.5 billion Apple sales in China, $19.2 billion should be attributed to Apple's activities in software, product design, brand promotion, system integration and other tasks. This $19.2 billion proxies the total value added of Apple's services and intellectual property sold to Chinese consumers in the form of physical products assembled in China (Xing, 2020b). However, no matter how much Chinese consumers spend on Apple products, the value added of Apple's intangible assets and services embedded in those products have not added even one dollar to US exports to China. This strange phenomenon points to the error inherent in the failure of trade statistics to include exports of factoryless American MNCs.

A critical issue is whether this $19.2 billion should be classified as a US export to China. Exports, defined as goods/services sold by one country to another country, are important for a national economy because they generate income and employment. Policy makers prefer exports to imports, simply because exports constitute income and employment for domestic economy. In terms of income generation, exports of the services attributed to intangible assets have the same function as exports of physical goods such as grain and cars. This $19.2 billion, the income Apple accrued by selling Chinese consumers the services including product design, software development, marketing, brand promotion, contributes to the paychecks of Apple's employees. It is a transaction between an American company and Chinese consumers, and therefore should be treated as a US export to China, regardless of whether or not those services cross US borders.

Table 4.3 displays 2015 US exports to China and the corresponding trade deficits. It also presents Apple's net sales in the Chinese market and the estimated value added captured by Apple from the sales. The value added that Apple accrued from the Chinese market was equivalent to 16.6 percent of the US exports to China in that year. If Apple's value added were taken into account,

Table 4.3 **Apple's sales in, and US trade with China, 2015 (Billions US dollar)**

	2015
US exports	115.9
US trade deficit	367.3
Apple sales	56.5
Apple value added	19.2
Apple value added/US exports (Percentage)	16.6
Apple value added/US trade deficit (Percentage)	5.2

Source: Xing (2020b).

US exports to China would rise by 16.6 percent, and the corresponding deficit would decrease by 5.2 percent. Recognizing the value added of Apple as part of US exports would narrow the trade gap between the US and China and mitigate the unprecedented bilateral trade imbalance. It is noteworthy that this potential revaluation is due to just one factoryless American company, namely, Apple. Many factoryless American MNCs operate in the same fashion. Bayard *et al.* (2015) reported that in 2012, 21 of the companies listed in the Standard and Poor's 500 Index, including AMD, Qualcomm, Cisco Systems, Apple and Nike, were exclusively engaged in factoryless manufacturing. If all the value added of the intellectual property and services embedded in their products, produced by foreign contract manufacturers, were recorded as part of US exports to China, China–US trade would be more balanced than indicated by current trade statistics.

As more and more American MNCs become factoryless, their international operations carry higher and higher weight in international trade relations. Analysis focusing solely on trade in goods and conventional service trade is misleading and tends to underestimate actual US exports, and in turn exaggerates its trade deficit. From the perspective of the bilateral trade between China and the US, especially when the trade balance is discussed (1) for either political or economic reasons; (2) in terms of who benefits and loses from the trade relations; or (3) to show how American MNCs have been benefiting from the fast-growing Chinese market, it is essential to take account of the value added gained by factoryless American MNCs in the Chinese market.

Here, I confine my analysis to American factoryless manufacturers rather than all American affiliates in China, because the value added of American affiliates in China includes wages paid to Chinese workers, rent for Chinese land, taxes paid to the Chinese government and profits reaped by American affiliates. It is wrong to argue that the value added of American affiliates in China should be considered as "an export of the US" to China, and even if we focus on after-tax profits of American affiliates in China, it is still questionable to classify after-tax profits as investment income or income arising from intangible assets such as brands. American affiliates in China create jobs for the Chinese economy, but American factoryless manufacturers generally have no greenfield investment in China and create little if any employment there, since their production is done by contract manufacturers, and non-production work is done mainly by employees in the home country.

Conclusion

Trade with China accounts for virtually half of the US trade deficit in goods. The low savings rate of American households, China's tariff and non-tariff barriers, and the dominance of the US dollar in global trade cannot fully explain the extraordinarily heavy weighting of the US trade deficit toward China. The inappropriateness of the current (outdated) trade statistics methodology to the evaluation of value chain-based modern trade substantially inflates the US trade deficit with China. After China became a member of the WTO, many MNCs from developed countries have integrated China into their value chains, allocating assembly and other low-skill tasks to Chinese firms. Furthermore, most Chinese exports to the US are made of intermediates imported from third countries. The value added of the iPhone X assembled in China is 75 percent foreign, whereas other electronics, computers and optical products contain 54 percent foreign value added. On average, foreign value added makes up 33.9 percent of Chinese exports to the US in 2015. Conventional trade statistics unambiguously exaggerate Chinese exports and hence China's trade surplus with the US, since they implicitly assume that all value added of exports belongs to the exporting nation. A country of origin breakdown of the value added of Chinese exports to the US shows that, to a large extent, China's surplus with the US should be considered as a surplus between the US and each of the countries involved in the value chains that manufacture Chinese exports.

It is most encouraging that economists primarily agree that domestic value added in exports is a better measure for accurate evaluation of the bilateral trade balance between China and the US. Value added in trade is not a simple economic concept; it has very important implications for evaluation of bilateral payments associated with trade flows. In general, it is the lead firms of GVCs, not assemblers/manufacturers, who pay suppliers directly for their parts and services. Exports and import statistics do not necessarily reflect inflows and outflows of income via value chain trade. It is misleading to use gross value of trade to gauge the status of bilateral payments. In the era of GVCs, trade in value added is the most appropriate parameter for evaluation of the balance of payments associated with external trade flows.

The international division of labor along the lines of production of two different products is a classic trade model found in standard economic textbooks. The proliferation of GVCs has given rise to a new international division of labor, along the value chain of the same product. More and more American MNCs, taking advantage of their comparative advantage in creating intangible assets, have specialized in research and development, product design, brand development, marketing and other services, outsourcing product manufacturing and assembly to foreign companies. They sell foreign consumers the value added of their intellectual property and services, embedded in tangible products assembled and/or manufactured by foreign contract manufacturers. This is a new type of trade. First, it does not cross American borders. Second, and more important, the intangible assets and services are embedded in physical products, and factoryless American MNCs can only realize gains after the physical products are sold to foreign users. American customs officers cannot trace those export activities or record them as part of US exports. If we rely solely on conventional trade statistics recorded by customs, US exports are definitely underestimated.

China has become the largest overseas market for many factoryless American MNCs, notably Apple, Nike, Qualcomm and AMD. All those factoryless companies have garnered tremendous revenue from the Chinese market by selling the services of intangible assets to Chinese consumers. Due to the inappropriateness of outdated statistical methodology for measuring value chain based trade, trade statistics do not record the export activities of factoryless American MNCs as part of American exports. The value added derived by Apple and other factoryless American MNCs constitute "missing exports" of the US. The failure of trade statistics to capture the exports of intangible assets by factoryless American MNCs has further widened the US trade deficit with China. Current trade statistics methodology is not appropriate for the assessment of trade dominated by GVCs. For an accurate understanding of how trade benefits all countries involved, especially countries specializing in brands, marketing, technological innovation and services, it is essential to reform trade statistics methodology so as to account for the value added of factoryless manufacturers derived from intellectual property and services embedded in their physical products sold in the global market.

Chapter 5

Diminished Impact of the Yuan Exchange Rate on Trade Balances

China's trade surplus soared after the country's accession to the World Trade Organization (WTO). During the period 2000–2007, it rose more than 10-fold and skyrocketed to $264 billion from $24 billion. Many scholars hold that the undervalued Chinese yuan contributed to China's trade surplus, in particular its trade surplus with the US. Goldstein and Lardy (2009) argued that during the period 2002–2008 the real Chinese yuan exchange rate was about 20 percent below its equilibrium level, which drove the surge of the Chinese current account surplus. Thorbecke (2006) estimated that the long-run Chinese yuan exchange rate coefficients for exports and imports between China and the US were both approximately equal to one. He concluded that if the Chinese yuan had appreciated 10 percent against the US dollar in 2005, the trade imbalance between the two countries would have decreased from 11 percent to 10 percent of the Chinese gross domestic product (GDP). Nobel laureate Paul Krugman openly accused the Chinese government of deliberately keeping the Chinese yuan undervalued so as to subsidize Chinese exports. He claimed that the distortionary exchange rate policy threatened the recovery of the global economy and called for a 25 percent across-the-board tariff on Chinese goods to force the Chinese government to change its exchange rate policy (Krugman, 2010).

The debate over Chinese exchange rate policy reached a climax after the eruption of the global financial crisis. Much of the debate over global imbalances, allegedly a root cause of the global financial crisis, focused on China's exchange rate regime. The undervalued Chinese yuan was regarded as a significant cause of global imbalances, in particular America's large current account deficit and China's blooming trade surplus (Obstfeld and Rogoff, 2009). The consensus view was that China's policy of rigid pegging to the dollar constituted a substantial real undervaluation of the Chinese yuan, and that undervaluation boosted China's trade surplus, which widened global imbalances, in turn triggering the global financial crisis (Cline, 2010). Former US Federal Reserve Chairman Bernanke (2009) suggested that the "saving glut" in the surplus countries, notably China, was recycled into US financial markets. This inflow of foreign savings resulted in a prolonged period of low interest rates in the US, creating incentives for aggressive searches for yields and encouraging reckless investment in risky housing-related assets such as subprime mortgages, which eventually fostered asset bubbles in the US and sowed the seeds of the global financial crisis.

However, McKinnon (2010) refuted the claim that the Chinese government had manipulated the yuan exchange rate, making the case that rather than deliberately undervaluing the yuan to gain a mercantile advantage, China had in fact been striving to achieve exchange rate and price stability. McKinnon considered the trade imbalance between the US and China a net saving imbalance, not an exchange rate phenomenon.

GDP identity is the theoretical starting point of macroeconomists' discussions of global imbalances and the magical power of exchange rate adjustments. In open macroeconomics, exchange rates and the prices of exports and imports lie at the center of academic and policy analysis. Exchange rates are thought to play a crucial role in determining a country's competitiveness in the global economy; its trade balance; its current account balance. According to conventional open macroeconomic models, if a country's currency appreciates, its exports become more expensive in terms of foreign currencies, and as a result foreign demand decreases, while imports become cheaper in terms of the national currency, and consequently the domestic demand for them increases. Therefore, the trade surplus shrinks, so does the current account surplus. However, the assumptions and conclusions of open macroeconomic models regarding the nexus between exchange rates and trade flows suit the classic cloth for wine trade, not value chain trade. The absence of microfoundations is a critical weakness of these macroeconomic analyses of global imbalances.

The conventional characterization of the nexus between exchange rates and trade is based on two outdated assumptions: that the entire value added of a country's exports is produced domestically; and that all imports exclusively serve domestic consumption and investment — which imply that if the home country's currency appreciates against that of the foreign country, the cost of materials, intermediates and services employed for manufacturing exports will be expected to rise proportionally in terms of the foreign currency. These simplistic assumptions do not hold for value chain trade, where exports generally contain a significant portion of imported materials and parts. Regardless of whether exporting firms have the monopolistic power to engage in exchange rate pass-through, the appreciation of a single currency has a very limited effect on the cost of products manufactured and distributed by GVCs. In the case of China, the pass-through effect of yuan exchange rates is generally discounted by the share of foreign value added embedded in Chinese exports. Additionally, imports used as inputs of manufacturing exports are not part of home country demand, but foreign demand. They may decrease rather than increase as the home country currency appreciates. The exchange rate elasticity of imports is also weakened in value chain trade. Furthermore, a value chain typically involves many firms located in a number of countries. The lead firm of the value chain usually chooses an anchor currency such as the US dollar for the pricing of parts and services for all firms involved in the chain, and settles all transactions among the firms in the anchor currency. In such a case, the pass-through effect of exchange rates is close to zero. In that sense, the conventional mechanism of exchange rates transmitted via export and import prices has been significantly undermined by the growing presence of value chain trade.

In Chapter 3, I showed that most Chinese exports occur via value chain trade. A decomposition of China's trade surplus reveals in more details the central role of value chain trade in the formation of Chinese trade surplus. During each year of the period 1994–2008, processing trade — a typical form of value chain trade, contributed virtually 100 percent of China's trade surplus. For example, in 2008, the year the global financial crisis erupted, China's trade surplus amounted to $298 billion, of which $297 billion was attributable to processing trade, even though processing exports accounted for less than 60 percent of China's total exports that year (Xing, 2012). The dominance of value chain trade in China's trade surplus suggests that yuan appreciation cannot function as a magic wand for lowering the surplus as expected by conventional wisdom. A clear understanding of those changes is indispensable for prescribing policy options to rebalance the global economy. In this chapter, I use the example of iPhone trade in the analysis of why, when value chain trade is dominant, yuan appreciation cannot have the expected impact on China's exports and trade balances. Symmetrically, the effectiveness of yuan depreciation in reducing the cost of Chinese exports in terms of the US dollar has also been weakened by the dominance of value chain trade. This makes it difficult for China to deliberately devalue the yuan for fighting the ongoing trade war with the US. I employ the iPhone X and simulation results to demonstrate the impossibility of using yuan depreciation to hedge the Trump tariffs. Even though the pass-through effect of yuan exchange rates has been undermined by the extensive presence of value chains, variation in yuan exchange rates could determine Chinese firms' entry into or exit from low-skilled and labor-intensive segments of value chains, thus indirectly impacting China's trade flows and balances. This chapter closes with a discussion of a new channel via which exchange rates affect value chain trade.

Yuan appreciation only affects Chinese value added: The case of iPhone trade

To a large extent, the share of foreign value added embedded in Chinese exports determines the effectiveness of yuan appreciation in reducing Chinese exports and trade surplus. Generally, the higher the share of foreign value added, the lower the expected effectiveness of yuan appreciation. The example of iPhone trade offers an intuitive explanation of how foreign value added can weaken the power of yuan appreciation to reduce China's exports and its trade surplus. Chapter 4 reveals that the iPhone 3G assembled in China costs $179, of which $6.50 is the Chinese value added in terms of assembly by Chinese workers, the remainder being the sum of the costs of parts made in foreign countries. If the Chinese yuan appreciated 50 percent against the US dollar, the cost of assembly by Chinese workers would increase by only $3.25 to $9.25, because the cost of all imported parts for the iPhone 3G is independent of that appreciation and should remain unchanged. Thus, that 50 percent yuan appreciation would raise the production cost of the iPhone 3G to $182.25, a mere 1.8 percent higher than the original $179 before the appreciation.

Compared with the $500 retail price, the $3.25 increase would be too small to justify an upward adjustment of the retail price of the iPhone. This means that the pass-through effect of a 50 percent yuan appreciation on the retail price paid by American consumers would be zero. Hence, even a 50 percent appreciation of the yuan would make no dent at all in China's iPhone exports to the US. This is not just a hypothetical projection. In 2017, China exported 42 million iPhones to the US, quadruple the 2009 volume, despite the steady real appreciation of the yuan against the US dollar. The rapid growth of Chinese iPhone exports to the US since the launch of the iPhone, is unambiguous evidence of a disconnect between yuan exchange rates and flows of value chain trade.

On the other hand, according to the conventional theory regarding the nexus between exchange rates and exports, yuan appreciation will increase the costs of both assembly service and all required parts, regardless of whether they are produced by China or supplied by other countries. Following that logic, if the exchange rate pass-through were 100 percent, a 50 percent appreciation of the yuan would raise the total production cost of the iPhone 3G by $89.50 and lift the production cost of the iPhone 3G assembled in China to $268.50, a significant jump in unit production cost that would warrant either a proportional upward adjustment of the retail price of the iPhone, or replacement of China as the assembler of iPhones with another low-cost country. Whether Apple raised the retail price or shifted the assembly out of China to cope with the assumed 50 percent appreciation of the yuan, China's iPhone exports to the US would surely fall. This conclusion, however, is based on an incorrect assumption about value chain trade.

In debates about global imbalances, virtually all macroeconomists, believing that the appreciation of the yuan could magically reduce China's trade surplus, in particular its trade surplus with the US, were in fact implicitly assuming that China contributed 100 percent of the gross value of Chinese exports. Figure 5.1 compares two estimates of the outcome of a 50 percent nominal appreciation of the yuan against the US dollar on the cost of the iPhone 3G assembled in China, assuming 100 percent pass-through. The left bar in

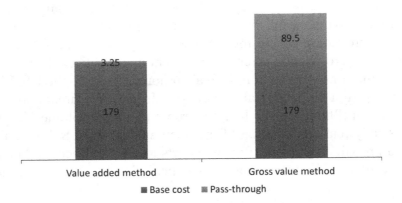

Figure 5.1   Expected impact of a 50 percent yuan appreciation on the iPhone 3G assembled in China (US dollar)

Source: The author's calculation, based on Xing and Detert (2010).

the figure represents the result of calculation with only the Chinese value added; the bar on the right shows the result of calculation based on total production cost of the phone. Clearly, the $3.25 estimate based on Chinese value added (the actual impact of the 50 percent appreciation of the yuan on the cost of the iPhone 3G) is much smaller than the $89.5 increase expected under the GVC — irrelevant assumption that the cost of all imported parts would rise proportionally.

For assembly of the iPhone 3G, China imported parts from at least nine firms in five different countries. An interesting question is whether the exchange rates between the yuan and the currencies of those five countries would affect the cost of the iPhone and thus impact Chinese iPhone exports to the US. Some studies (e.g., Adler *et al.*, 2019) suggest that the competitiveness of a country's exports is also affected by the appreciation/depreciation of its currency against the currencies of the countries that supply intermediate inputs. Theoretically, this may be a plausible scenario, but in reality, it is unrealistic on two counts. First, the lead firm of a GVC generally selects an anchor currency for the invoicing of all transactions along the value chain so as to reduce transaction costs and avoid exchange rate volatility. Second, the lead firm purchases directly from all suppliers and designates where those parts and components should be shipped to. In other words, the firms in charge of assembly of final products do not have to purchase necessary parts with their own financial resources. In the case of the iPhone, all components and services needed are priced in the US dollar. It is the Apple, not the Chinese assemblers, who purchases those parts and components and has them sent to China. The bilateral exchange rate between the Chinese yuan and the Japanese yen or the yuan and the Korean won, is irrelevant to the cost of Apple products assembled in China, and therefore cannot affect the export of iPhones from China to the US. This is true for all Apple products, iPhones, iMacs, iPad and iPods, which are assembled in China and exported to the rest of the world — and it is also true for all Chinese processing exports. The same reasoning can be applied to all Chinese exports that use imported parts priced in an anchor currency.

If all foreign-made intermediates are priced in an anchor currency when they enter and leave China, bilateral exchange rates between the Chinese yuan and the currencies of the countries who supply intermediate inputs used in Chinese exports are irrelevant and do not affect China's exports.

Country origin analysis of China's processing trade uncovered that 77 percent of China's processing imports came from East Asian economies such as Japan, Taiwan and Korea, while more than 70 percent of China's processing exports were destined for markets outside of East Asia (Xing, 2012). Realizing that the appreciation of the yuan alone may not be an effective tool for reducing the trade imbalance between the US and China, Thorbecke and Smith (2010) proposed a joint appreciation of East Asian currencies against the US dollar for the reduction of global imbalances, and argued that a joint appreciation of East Asian currencies would be a more effective means of reducing China's trade surplus than a unilateral appreciation of the yuan. In the 1980s, the Plaza Accord, signed by Japan, West Germany, UK, France, and the US, orchestrated a joint appreciation against the US dollar, but how much that appreciation reduced Japanese current account surplus remains a subject of debates. A coordinated joint appreciation of East Asian currencies against the US dollar might be just a hypothesis rooted in theory.

Additionally, a large portion of Chinese imports serves foreign demand, not China's domestic demand. This is another reason why the impact of the yuan exchange rate on Chinese trade balances has lessened. China, as the global assembly center, in 2018 imported $470 billion in parts and components (equivalent to 22 percent of Chinese total imports for that year) for the manufacture of exports; it imported $230 billion in integrated circuits: more than half of those items were re-exported as part of finished personal computers, mobile phones and other ICT products. This kind of imports represents foreign demand, not Chinese domestic demand. Such imports do not respond in the traditional fashion to the movement of exchange rates (i.e., they do not increase in volume as the yuan appreciates and decrease as the yuan depreciates). Theoretically speaking, if Chinese processing exports are to fall because of appreciation of the yuan, processing imports should fall too. An empirical investigation of the exchange rate elasticity of processing trade, analyzing panel data covering more than 100 of China's trading partners during 1992–2012, found that a 10 percent real appreciation of the Chinese yuan against the US dollar would give rise not only to a 9 percent decrease in processing exports, but also to a 5 percent fall in processing imports. Therefore, it is uncertain whether the appreciation of the yuan could significantly boost China's imports, especially when processing imports account for a very large portion of China's imports (Xing, 2012).

With regard to the reduction of trade surpluses, the Marshall–Lerner condition holds that an exchange rate appreciation will reduce trade surplus as long as the sum of the price elasticities of exports and imports is greater than one. One of the assumptions of the Marshall Lerner condition is that imports have a positive correlation to the appreciation of home country currency. As mentioned earlier, processing trade contributed more than 100 percent to the Chinese overall trade surplus. Reducing the trade surplus generated by processing trade is a key to rebalancing Chinese trade. Whether the appreciation of the yuan could lower the processing trade surplus, this would determine the effectiveness of yuan appreciation for mitigation of China's overall trade surplus. As emphasized earlier, Chinese processing imports would be expected to decrease by 5 percent for a 10 percent real appreciation; in this case, the Marshall Lerner condition does not hold and the surplus of China's processing trade would not fall. Cheung *et al.* (2015) calculated the exchange rate elasticities of China's processing trade with the US; they estimated that processing imports would increase by 5 percent for a one percent real appreciation of the yuan, while processing exports would decrease by 1.87 percent. Based on these estimates, they concluded that the Marshall Lerner condition did in fact hold for processing trade between the US and China. However, the highly elastic and positive relation between yuan appreciation and China's processing import volume unambiguously refutes the characterization of processing imports, which are employed in the manufacture of processing exports, not for Chinese domestic consumption or investment.

General studies on countries other than China also find empirical evidence supporting the hypothesis that GVCs have substantially mitigated the impact of exchange rates on trade flow. Powers and Riker (2013) investigated the exchange rate elasticity of Chinese exports to the US and found that it would be significantly smaller if the exports were measured in Chinese value added rather than gross value. Ahmed *et al.* (2015) estimated the impact of changes in real exchange rate on export volumes for a sample of 46 countries during the period 1996–2012, and concluded that on average, GVC participation reduced the elasticity of manufacturing exports to real effective exchange rates (REERs) by 22 percent, and by close to 30 percent for countries with the highest rates of GVC participation. The REER, based on gross trade volumes and consumer price indices, is a parameter used widely in economic analysis for evaluation of country competitiveness. However, REER is not compatible with value chain trade. Bems and Johnson (2012) proposed a value-added REER, where the weights of trading partners are determined by bilateral trade in value added. They suggested that as value-added REER takes GVCs into account in assessments of competitiveness, it could be used as an alternative to REER for evaluation of the impact of exchange rates on the comparative advantage of countries participating in value chains.

Yuan depreciation to offset Trump's tariffs: Mission impossible

The ongoing US–China trade war constitutes a new scenario where the standard textbook theory on exchange rates and trade flows is no longer valid. President Trump had been using tariffs as a weapon for the waging of a trade war with China. Indisputably, the 25 percent tariff levied on $250 billion in Chinese goods has artificially raised the cost of Chinese exports and undermined the competitiveness of made in China products in the US market. When the trade war started in March of 2018, the exchange rate was 6.2 yuan/

dollar. Since then, the yuan had gradually depreciated; by the beginning of August 2019, the exchange rate had risen to 7.03 yuan/dollar, a 13.4 percent nominal depreciation of the yuan against the dollar. This significant depreciation clearly clashed with the People's Bank of China's policy of maintaining stable yuan exchange rates. There was speculation that the Chinese government deliberately allowed the depreciation as a defense against US tariff attacks. As soon as the yuan surpassed the 7 yuan per dollar level in August 2019, US Department of Treasury (2019) designated China as a currency manipulator.

In the classic cloth for wine trade, currency depreciation can handily counterbalance tariff burdens. This might lead one to believe that a 25 percent yuan depreciation against the dollar could completely offset the 25 percent tariff imposed by the Trump administration. However, this is not so straightforward in the case of value chain trade. Foreign materials and intermediates embedded in Chinese exports not only substantially erode the effect of yuan depreciation but also greatly amplify the tariff burden. First, the depreciation of the yuan can only lower the costs of Chinese made materials, parts and services in terms of the US dollar. Foreign intermediates embedded in Chinese exports are independent of yuan depreciation. It is erroneous to assume that a 25 percent depreciation of the yuan could result in a proportional fall in the costs of Chinese exports measured in the US dollar. In general, the higher the foreign value added embedded in Chinese exports, the lower the effect of yuan depreciation. Second, when US Customs taxes Chinese imports, the gross value of Chinese products is taken as the tax base. In other words, not only is Chinese value added subject to the Trump tariffs but foreign value added, inherent in the foreign parts shipped to China for assembly into final products, is subject to those tariffs as well. In this scenario, the tariff burden is actually amplified, which makes offsetting the negative impact of the tariffs by means of yuan depreciation even more challenging.

Here, I take up the case of the iPhone X to demonstrate why the depreciation of the yuan cannot hedge the risk posed by the Trump tariffs. As explained in Chapter 4, the total production cost of the iPhone X is $409.25, of which $104 is attributed to Chinese parts and assembly service, with the rest stemming from the components imported from foreign countries. If the iPhone X assembled in China were subject to a 25 percent tariff, the tariff base would be $409.25 and Apple would have to pay $102.30 in tariffs for each iPhone X imported to the US. The parts supplied by companies in Japan, Korea, the US and other countries would be taxed simply on the basis that they were shipped to China for final assembly. This value chain phenomenon multiplies the detrimental impact of the Trump tariffs on Chinese goods. On the other hand, if only the Chinese value added of $104 were taxed at 25 percent, the tariff burden would be just $26, about one-fourth of the tariff on the gross value. In fact, the $102.30 tariff is equivalent to a tariff of almost 100 percent calculated using the Chinese value added. Figure 5.2 compares two different calculations of the tariff burden on the iPhone X. The left bar represents the calculation based on the Chinese value added; the right is based on the gross value. The difference between the two is $76.3, about 18.6 percent of the total production cost.

As outlined previously, the foreign parts cause the tariff burden to increase significantly. However, the depreciation of the yuan can only affect the cost of Chinese parts and services. Specifically, a

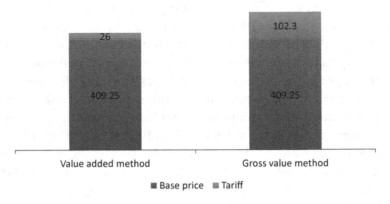

Figure 5.2   Impact of a 25 percent tariff on the iPhone X assembled in China (US dollar)

Source: Calculation by the author, based on Xing (2020a).

25 percent depreciation of the yuan could lower the dollar cost of Chinese parts and services proportionally, and thus completely counterbalance the negative impact of the 25 percent tariff on the Chinese inputs. On the other hand, the cost of foreign parts would remain unchanged regardless of the extent of yuan depreciation. The tariff burden due to the foreign parts is estimated here at $76.30. Theoretically, it might be possible to offset the $76.30 tariff burden if the yuan depreciated by 400 percent against the US dollar, large enough to wreak economic havoc in China, the second largest economy in the world. The case of the iPhone X is a good intuitive illustration of how the foreign materials and parts embedded in Chinese exports mitigate the expected effect of yuan depreciation; it suggests that it is almost impossible to hedge the risk of the Trump tariffs by means of yuan depreciation when value chains dominate China's trade with the US.

Generally, the share of foreign value added embedded in Chinese exports determines the extent to which yuan depreciation could mitigate the negative impact of the Trump tariffs. My simulation results show that: (1) the percentage of yuan depreciation required is always higher than the corresponding tariff when foreign value added is not zero; and (2) it rises rapidly as the ratio of foreign value added increases. Figure 5.3 depicts the percentage of yuan

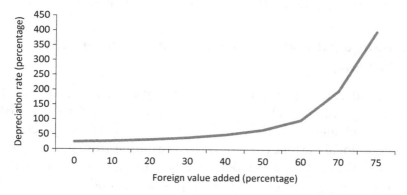

Figure 5.3 Yuan depreciation required to offset a 25 percent US tariff

Source: Xing (2020a).

depreciation required to offset completely the negative impact of a 25 percent tariff for selected ratios of foreign value added. When foreign value added is zero, a 25 percent depreciation would be sufficient to offset the tariff; if the share of foreign value added contained in Chinese exports is 30 percent, at least 40 percent depreciation of the yuan would be necessary. The required yuan depreciation rises sharply after the ratio of foreign value added exceeds half of the gross value of Chinese exports. If foreign value added accounts for 60 percent, the yuan would have to depreciate by 100 percent in order to counterbalance the tariff; a 200 percent depreciation would be required for the case of 70 percent foreign value added. In 2015, Chinese exports to the US contained an average of 33.9 percent foreign value added, which would require a 43.4 percent depreciation of the yuan to completely offset the negative impact of the 25 percent tariff. The simulation results demonstrate that the required depreciation is too high to be achieved by means of Chinese government intervention in foreign exchange markets. It is virtually impossible for the Chinese government to hedge the risk of the 25 percent tariff currently imposed on $250 billion in Chinese goods. From the GVC perspective, this reasoning explains why some multinational corporations (MNCs) which had been outsourcing products from China, or manufacturing products in China for the US market, have shifted their supply chains out of China in order to avoid the US–China trade war.

Exchange rate transmission channel under value chain trade

Traditionally, export and import prices have been regarded as the channel by which exchange rates determine trade flows and balances. Exchange rate pass-through is defined as the percentage change in local currency import prices resulting from a one percent change in the exchange rate between the currencies of the exporting and importing countries. If import prices respond one-for-one to exchange rate variation, the pass-through will be 100 percent. A scenario in which import prices only partially reflect changes in exchange rates is referred to as incomplete exchange rate pass-through (Goldberg and Knetter, 1997). Exporters can set prices in their own currencies (referred to in the literature as producer currency pricing, or PCP); in the currencies of destination markets (known as local currency pricing, LCP); or in vehicle currencies. Currency invoicing choices affect the degree of pass-through effect (Goldberg and Tille, 2005). Theoretically speaking, if exporters opt for PCP, variations in exchange rate can be fully transmitted into import price fluctuations. On the other hand, under LCP, import prices are independent of exchange rate movement, at least in the short run (Engel, 2006). It is expected that a change in import prices would affect trade flow, given the substitutability between imports and domestically produced products. The effect of yuan revaluation on China's trade balance is determined by two kinds of elasticity: price-exchange rate elasticity and quantity–price elasticity. The former measures pass-through effects of exchange rates on the price of both imports and exports; the latter measures changes in import and export quantities in response to price changes. Pass-through effects represent the first step in a chain reaction from nominal exchange rate adjustments to eventual changes in exports, imports and balance of trade.

Chinese firms primarily participate in GVCs through three channels: (1) assembly of products for GVC lead firms; (2) supply of parts for upstream foreign firms or local firms who are OEMs of MNCs; and (3) supply of finished products to foreign brand marketers or large retailers. These firms' exports are generally priced in an anchor currency, in most cases the US dollar. As a result, there is no mechanism by which these Chinese firms can pass the effect of yuan appreciation on to their foreign buyers. In addition, Chinese firms participating in GVCs are designated suppliers of GVC lead firms; their relationship with the lead firms is defined by contracts, rather than by random buyer–seller relations in markets. The binding contracts mean that (1) prices of parts and services provided by Chinese firms cannot be re-negotiated because of short-term exchange rate movements; and (2) unless Chinese firms have monopolistic power over their products and services, they cannot pass on the cost of yuan appreciation through renegotiations. For example, no Chinese suppliers can negotiate prices with Walmart or Apple. Hence, there is no mechanism for the transmission of yuan appreciation to prices of the Chinese exports, which depend on GVCs. In other words, the exchange rate elasticity of Chinese value chain based exports is virtually zero.

For value chain trade, the transmission channel of variations in yuan exchange rates is not the price of Chinese exports, but Chinese firms' entry into and exit from GVCs operated by foreign MNCs. Cost-saving is one of the major motivations for MNCs to offshore low-skilled tasks to, or outsource cheap products and services from China. The depreciation of the yuan lowers the cost of Chinese labor in terms of the US dollar and makes China an attractive location for low value added, labor-intensive tasks. This depreciation also increases the relative wealth of foreign investors. From the point of the view of foreign investors with capital valued in the US dollar, all production inputs in China (e.g., labor, land, machines and assets) become cheaper after yuan devaluation, which encourages these investors to conduct greenfield investment in China.

Foreign direct investment (FDI) has served as a major means of integrating China into GVCs. China has been the largest recipient of FDI among developing countries. Until recently the majority of FDI in China, in particular FDI from Taiwan, Hong Kong, Japan and Korea, had been export oriented. The cumulative depreciation of the yuan from the late 1980s to the early 2000s was one of the major determinants of FDI inflows into China, which subsequently transformed China into the global center of manufacturing assembly. To a large extent, China's close integration into GVCs can be attributed to massive inflows of FDI, driven by the sharp devaluation of the Chinese yuan from 1989 onward due to the transition of China's exchange rate regime from the dual exchange rate system to a unified single exchange rate system. The nominal yuan–dollar exchange rate rose sharply, from 3.76 in November 1989 to 8.62 in January 1994, a nominal 56 percent devaluation of the yuan. Subsequently, the Chinese government had followed dollar peg policy and essentially maintained a fixed exchange rate to the dollar from then to 2005 (Xing, 2006a).

This sharp devaluation dramatically enhanced China's competitiveness as a global production base, against not only FDI source countries but also countries competing with China for FDI, including Malaysia, Thailand, Indonesia and the Philippines, all major recipients of Japanese FDI in Asia prior to 1990. However, in the wake of the depreciation of the yuan in the early 1990s, China became the largest recipient of Japanese FDI in Asia. In 1995, Japanese FDI to China accounted for 43 percent of all Japanese FDI in Asia, much higher than the 1990 figure of 5.3 percent. Because the currencies of Indonesia, Malaysia and the Philippines were at that time pegged to the US dollar, the cumulative devaluation of the yuan against the dollar from 1989 onward resulted in a proportional depreciation of the yuan against the currencies of those four South-East Asian countries, which in turn triggered a shift of Japanese FDI away from those countries and toward China. At that time, aside from Hong Kong, Japan was the largest source of FDI in China, and most Japanese FDI to China was export oriented. In 2001, Japanese affiliates in China exported more than 65 percent of their outputs to overseas markets. The segmentation separating production location and product market confines the impact of the devaluation to local production costs and does not touch sales prices in the global market. Therefore, export-oriented FDI benefited substantially from the currency devaluation of the yuan (Xing, 2006b).

In much the same way, the appreciation of the yuan after 2005 caused indigenous Chinese firms to exit from value chains, and MNCs to either shift their production facilities out of China or source products from countries other than China. The cumulative appreciation of the yuan since 2005 has unambiguously raised the cost of Chinese labor and greatly undercut Chinese competitiveness in assembly tasks against other developing countries such as India, Vietnam and Indonesia, who are also richly endowed with cheap labor. The significant decrease in China's processing trade with supplied materials is a clear evidence of that. Since the beginning of China's economic reforms, processing exports with supplied materials grew every year, peaking at \$116 billion in 2007 — and then began to decline, dropping to \$78 billion in 2017, which suggests that many Chinese firms had exited the pure assembly business of producing exports with supplied materials. Cumulative real appreciation of the yuan was one of the major factors prompting Chinese firms to exit pure assembly, the least value added segment of GVCs (Xing, 2018a).

A case in point: China used to be the largest assembly base for Samsung mobile phones. In 2012, about 65 percent of Samsung mobile phones were assembled in China. By 2019, Samsung had shifted all its Chinese assembly to Vietnam, transforming that country into the second largest mobile phone exporting nation in the world, after China. Increased labor cost, partially attributable to the appreciation of the yuan, is one of the major reasons for Samsung's relocation of its mobile phone value chains out of China. In a nutshell, the movement of yuan exchange rates has affected the value chain trade via Chinese firms' entry to and exit from GVCs, not the traditional price mechanism.

Conclusion

The dominance of GVCs in China's commodity trade with the rest of the world has dramatically diminished the impact of yuan exchange rates on China's exports and imports and on its balance of trade. If there is a pass-through effect and if the yuan is to appreciate, only the domestic value added of Chinese exports will be affected. The larger the share of foreign value added in Chinese exports, the smaller the exchange rate pass-through effect. Moreover, Chinese imports for manufacturing exports represent the demand from overseas markets and are not part of China's domestic demand — and they tend to decrease if Chinese processing exports fall because of yuan appreciation. Clearly, it is uncertain whether the appreciation of the yuan could reduce China's trade surplus as long as a large portion of Chinese trade is value chain trade. By the same logic, it is unrealistic to expect that yuan depreciation would be able to completely hedge the risk of the Trump tariffs. Foreign materials and parts included in Chinese exports not only amplify the negative impact of those tariffs, but also undermine the expected effect of yuan depreciation. It is mission impossible to use yuan depreciation to counterbalance the Trump administration's 25 percent tariff on Chinese goods.

Now, in the age of GVCs, export and import prices are no longer the main channel via which yuan exchange rates influence China's trade flows. Rather, the movement of yuan exchange rates decide Chinese firms' entry to or exit from GVCs, indirectly affecting China's trade flows and balances. The cumulative depreciation of the yuan in the 1990s greatly promoted the inflows of export-oriented FDI and enhanced China's competitiveness as a source of cheap, labor-intensive products, thus facilitating Chinese firms' participation in GVCs. On the other hand, the cumulative appreciation of the yuan since 2005 has induced (1) the exit of Chinese firms from assembly tasks, and (2) MNCs' relocation of labor-intensive tasks out of China.

Chapter 6

A Supportive Policy Environment: The Key to China's GVC Entry

The proliferation of global value chains (GVCs) in recent decades offers emerging economies a new path toward industrialization and economic development. With the extensive fragmentation of the manufacturing industry resulting from modularization, it is no longer necessary for a country to build production capacities for an entire industry in order to produce a final product. By taking part in value chains operated by multinational corporations (MNCs) of industrialized countries, developing countries can join high-technology value creation processes despite their limitations in capital and technology. In retrospect, China's export miracle over the last 40 years has been a story of success rooted in active participation in GVCs as a means of implementing export-led growth strategy and pursuing industrialization. However, for firms in developing countries, plugging into GVCs and taking advantage of the accompanying spillover effects is easier said than done. Entry into GVCs requires a supportive environment that encourages GVC lead firms to expand their value chains beyond national borders and facilitates the entry of domestic firms into value chains. Nurturing an environment that enables GVC participation requires, first and foremost, appropriate institutional arrangements, policies and regulations governing trade and foreign direct investment (FDI).

The 2015 OECD report (OECD, 2015), *Participation of Developing Countries in Global Value Chains: Trade and Trade Related Policies*, identifies trade policy elements such as low import tariffs in both home and foreign markets, and openness to inward FDI as crucial factors of supporting developing nations' participation in GVCs. *Asia-Pacific Trade and Investment Report 2015* (ESCAP, 2015) summarizes three policy elements necessary for the support of firm upgrading and GVC participation: (1) securing entry to GVCs; (2) expanding participation in GVCs; and (3) upgrading within GVCs. UNIDO (2019) lists incentives for promoting trade and FDI, infrastructure, labor skills and industrial clusters as important in this regard. *Global Value Chain Development Report 2017* (World Bank, 2017) emphasizes contract enforcement and intellectual property protection by institutions as essential elements for ensuring the reliable movement of supplies across national borders and the protection of intangible assets.

To transform China from an isolated and centrally planned economy to an open and market-oriented one, the Chinese government implemented a series of economic and institutional reforms over the last 40 years. Those reforms include price liberalization, state-owned enterprise reforms, fiscal reforms, trade liberalization, legislative reforms, and reforms of FDI policy (Chow, 1994; Lin *et al.*, 2003). Those reform initiatives, related to liberalization of trade and FDI, are the most important elements for fostering an environment supportive to Chinese companies' successful involvement in GVCs. In this chapter, I discuss three specific policies: (1) establishment of a processing trade regime; (2) promotion of inflows of FDI; and (3) accession to the World Trade Organization (WTO), and explain why those policies are essential for Chinese firms' participation in fragmented global production and for motivating MNCs to offshore their production activities to China.

Processing trade regime

Since the beginning of its economic reforms, the Chinese government has been aggressively promoting processing trade, in which

Chinese firms import some or all of requisite raw materials and intermediate inputs from abroad; process or assemble them into final products; and finally export those products. Processing trade is clearly a subset of GVC activities, and is generally labor intensive. For a country to engage in processing trade on a large scale requires a huge pool of cheap labor. In the early 1980s, with a population of 1.3 billion and average per capita income less than $1,000, China was an ideal candidate for foreign MNCs offshoring of assembly tasks and outsourcing of the manufacture of cheap, labor-intensive products. Specialization in processing trade was a right choice for Chinese firms; it enabled them to plug into value chains managed by foreign MNCs and leverage China's comparative advantage. Additionally, processing trade enabled Chinese firms to overcome the deficiency of the Chinese economy in terms of capacity to supply sufficient volumes of high-quality parts, weaknesses stemming from China's low level of industrialization and technology bottlenecks in the 1980s and 1990s.

There are two processing trade modalities: processing with supplied materials and processing with purchased materials. In the first modality, a foreign contractor supplies a Chinese company with all materials and intermediate inputs necessary for manufacturing products. The Chinese company receives processing fees after delivering the products that meet the pre-specified standards to the foreign contractor. Processing with supplied materials implies that upstream foreign firms simply outsource assembly tasks to Chinese firms; the contribution of the Chinese firms is simple labor service.

After its rapid economic growth of the last four decades, China has accumulated more than $3 trillion in foreign exchange reserves, the largest in the world. Back in the 1980s and 1990s, though, China was struggling with a shortage of foreign exchange reserves. It was difficult for Chinese firms to obtain hard currencies, such as US dollars, needed for importing production materials from abroad. Processing with supplied materials was a mechanism by which Chinese firms could overcome the liquidity constraint of foreign currencies; it allowed Chinese firms lacking foreign currencies to acquire foreign-made intermediate inputs for manufacturing exports.

In the second modality, processing with purchased materials, Chinese firms use foreign currencies to purchase raw materials and other intermediate inputs from abroad, then export the products made of the imported intermediates to GVC lead firms or foreign firms in the upper reaches of value chains. In the production of processing exports with purchased materials, it is a common practice to supplement imported intermediates with a relatively small amount of domestically produced inputs.

In order to promote its processing trade, the Chinese government has deliberately established a two-phase free trade regime for processing trade. First, Chinese firms qualified for conducting processing trade are exempted from tariffs and value-added taxes when they import materials and parts from abroad for the manufacture of exports, and their imports are not subject to import quotas. Second, their exports, usually referred as processing exports, are exempted from value-added and export taxes. Those preferential treatments have effectively cultivated a free trade regime for the processing trade. As MNCs outsource their production tasks to more and more countries, tariff and non-tariff barriers of the countries involved in GVCs definitely raise the transaction costs of GVC management. Trade facilitation and low- and non-tariff barriers are indispensable for a country attempting to join GVCs. Driven by abundant cheap labor, the processing trade regime has transformed China into an ideal location for foreign MNCs offshoring of the assembly of manufacturing products targeting international markets — one of main drivers of China's transformation into a world factory.

In tandem with those elements of preferential national policy governing processing trade, local Chinese governments have established processing export zones (PEZs) in bonded areas. They invested heavily in electricity, water supply, roads, office buildings, factories and other infrastructure necessary for smooth operations of factories inside PEZs. Before 2010 there were about 55 PEZs in China; they were constructed to serve as venues for firms specializing in processing trade, most of them foreign-invested enterprises (FIEs). Economic and technological development zones (ETDZs), used by local governments for industrial upgrading and the promotion of regional development, also enhanced the growth of processing trade. Before 2010, there were 33 ETDZs across the country, accounting for 12.8 percent of Chinese processing imports (intermediate inputs used for the manufacture of exports) (Yu and Tian, 2019).

Not only did the processing trade regime open a unique path for Chinese firms to participate in GVCs, it also encouraged MNCs to extend their value chains into China, and provided a unique channel by which MNCs could utilize China's abundant cheap labor. In the last 40 years, hundreds of thousands of investors from Hong Kong, Taiwan, Korea, Singapore, Japan, the US and European countries seized that opportunity and set up processing factories in China to serve non-Chinese markets. In the ICT industry, Taiwanese companies such as Foxconn, Pegatron and Compal Electronic (the world's leading original equipment manufacturers (OEMs) of electronics) had offshored virtually all their assembly facilities to Mainland China, which automatically created a bridge between China and global ICT value chains. Taiwan started to develop its semiconductor and information technology production capacity in the early 1980s. As ICT gradually matured and the processes for the production of ICT grew modularized, Taiwanese companies got involved in the fragmentation of the global ICT industry, working as OEMs for leading international ICT firms such as IBM, DELL, Intel and SONY.

To take advantage of low labor cost and the preferential policies for processing trade, Taiwanese companies gradually offshored most of their production capacity to Mainland China. This not only boosted China's output in ICT but also helped insert Chinese firms into ICT value chains. In 2007, in terms of global market share, Taiwanese companies ranked number one in laptop computer manufacture with more than 90 million units; in production of LCD PC monitors with 117.5 million units; and in motherboard fabrication with 149 million units — and ranked number two in desktop PCs, servers and digital cameras. Most of those ICT products were actually produced in Taiwanese factories located in Mainland China but sold in markets other than Taiwan and Mainland China. For instance, in 2007, 98 percent of digital cameras made by Taiwanese companies were in fact produced in Taiwanese factories in Mainland China; for laptop computers, the percentage was 97.5. By 2009, Taiwanese companies had offshored 95 percent of their ICT assembly capacity to Mainland China. Thanks to the Taiwanese company Foxconn, China has been the largest assembler of Apple products since the launch of the first generation iPhone (Xing, 2014).

The strategy of using processing trade as an inroad to promotion of exports and integration of the Chinese economy into GVCs has been very successful. As mentioned in Chapter 3, processing trade was a main driver of the Chinese export miracle. The share of processing exports in China's total exports rose from less than 10 percent in the early 1980s to a peak of 57 percent in 2006. In the category of high-technology products, where China even surpassed Japan, the US and the 27 EU countries in terms of export volume, processing exports accounted for more than 80 percent during the period 2000–2010, when Chinese exports were experiencing double-digit annual growth. Processing trade has served as a special vehicle for made in China products to penetrate international markets, in particular those of high-income countries. Before China's entry into the WTO, foreign goods were subject to prohibitively high tariffs for entering the Chinese market. Processing imports, on the other hand, have enjoyed zero tariffs. Indeed, China's maneuvering in this processing scenario represents an innovative strategy and a unique aspect of the Chinese export miracle.

FDI promotion strategy

The geographic dispersion of production activity across national borders is to a certain extent a result of MNCs' greenfield investment abroad, one popular mode of offshoring production. By investing in foreign subsidiaries, either to serve local markets or to build up export bases, MNCs extend their value chains beyond the borders of their home countries. Inflows of FDI, in particular export-oriented FDI, is always an igniter of the GVC participation trajectory for the hosting country: countries hosting MNCs' subsidiaries are automatically integrated into GVCs. Moreover, investment by foreign firms gives rise to opportunities for local firms to participate in value chains. It is common for FIEs to procure locally produced materials and parts. As a result, local firms have an opportunity to join GVCs as designated suppliers for foreign subsidiaries. For instance, some FIEs in China initially conducted pure assembly and imported all required materials and parts from abroad. As indigenous Chinese firms have gradually developed their technology capacity and mastered the skills for production of high-quality substitutes for imported parts, those FIEs have begun turning to qualified local Chinese firms for parts and services. Hence, the presence of FIEs has constituted a window of opportunity for local Chinese firms to become involved in value chains operated by foreign MNCs. Empirical evidence shows a close relationship between FDI and GVC participation. In its analysis of 20 years of data for 187 countries, UNCTAD (2013) found a significant positive correlation between annual GVC participation growth and annual growth of inward FDI stock, which indicates that FDI volume may be an important determinant of the degree of a country's involvement in GVCs. It was estimated that for some countries in South-East Asia, FDI openness increased the GVC participation rate by over 20 percentage points (Kowalski *et al.*, 2015).

Coordinated FDI policy is indispensable for the success of the processing trade. Since the beginning of China's economic reforms, the processing trade regime has been intertwined with China's FDI promotion strategy. Facing a severe shortage of financial resources and constrained by inefficient stated-owned enterprises, the Chinese government was determined to make use of FDI so as to offset capital deficiencies; acquire advanced technology and production know-how; promote exports. As the Chinese government kicked off its revolutionary economic reforms in 1978, it placed a top priority on opening China to FDI. This was both an economic decision and a bold political move, since historically foreign investment and foreign ownership in Chinese territory had been regarded as synonymous with foreign colonial rule.

In 1979, the Chinese government promulgated a law on Chinese-foreign joint ventures so as to eliminate institutional hurdles and establish a legal environment for the protection of the interests of foreign investors. The Chinese government followed a gradual rather than big-bang approach in its implementation of economic reforms, referred to by chief architect Deng Xiaoping as "crossing the river by feeling the stones." Being cautious and uncertain about the consequences of opening China to the rest of the world, the Chinese government initially limited foreign investment to Shantou, Shenzhen, Zhuhai and Xiamen, the four special economic zones (SEZs) set up as experimental sites in 1980. In 1984, following the success of the four SEZs in attracting FDI, promoting exports and boosting regional economic growth, the Chinese government decided to expand special economic zones by including 14 coastal cities. In 1986, to give foreign investors more choices and greater autonomy the Chinese government passed a law on wholly foreign-owned enterprises, which officially permits foreign investors to set up and operate companies independently. Eventually, in the late 1990s, the whole of China was opened to foreign investment.

Preferential tax policies were major instruments employed to incentivize foreign investment. Before the Chinese government unified its tax codes for domestic companies and FIEs in 2005, FIEs enjoyed a substantial array of preferential tax treatments. For instance, FIEs were exempted from income tax for two years after first realization of profit, and were eligible for a 50 percent reduction in tax liability for three years after that (Zebregs and Tseng, 2002). The goals of MNCs' engagement in greenfield investment abroad include the occupation of local markets and the use of host countries as export platforms. One of the main forms of FDI, export-oriented FDI, promotes the exports of FDI host countries substantially. At that time the Chinese government was mainly targeting export-oriented FDI in its promotion of employment and economic growth. To encourage the inflow of export-oriented FDI, the Chinese government extended the initial five-year, 50 percent discount in income tax, applicable to FIEs that exported more than 70 percent of their output to overseas markets. In addition, the Chinese government required FIEs to be independent in terms of foreign currencies needed for imports. This policy deliberately steered FIEs toward the export of a large portion of their output to overseas markets.

Since the beginning of the economic reforms, economic growth has been the most important yardstick for the evaluation of the performance of Chinese local government officials and decisions regarding promotions up the bureaucratic hierarchy. Regarding competition for FDI, in addition to the preferential tax policies permitted by the central government, local governments offered a variety of incentives to foreign investors. For example, the finance department of Guangdong, the largest province in terms of exports, offered foreign investors cash rewards for projects in which they invested more than $50 million, amounting to at least 2 percent of the investment. Land is another enticement to foreign investment: Chinese local governments have the authority to acquire farm land and convert it into industrial land. They usually solicit foreign investment by means of that cheaply acquired industrial land. For example, in Guangdong, foreign investors in the manufacturing industry can lease industrial land for 70 percent of the lowest rent. Also, certified foreign senior managers of FIEs can enjoy the same privileges as local residents in terms of social insurance, healthcare, house purchases, banking services and children's education (*China Daily*, 2019).

Thanks to those policies in tandem with its abundant cheap labor and rapidly growing economy, China has been very successful in attracting FDI. Cumulative FDI in China for the period 1980–2018 amounted to $2.1 trillion, making China the largest recipient of FDI among all developing countries (*Xinhua News*, 2019). The massive inflows of FDI have provided crucial support for the growth of the processing trade and exports. Figure 6.1 presents the involvement of FIEs in China's exports from 1995 to 2018. In 1995, exports by FIEs accounted for 31.2 percent of total Chinese exports; by 2006 that figure had risen to a peak of 58.2 percent, more than half of China's total exports.

Since 2010, the export share of FIEs had gradually declined. It dropped to 41.7 percent in 2018. The shift of FIE orientation from exports to the domestic market is one of the factors responsible for that long-term decrease. China's rapid economic growth has led to an ongoing expansion of its domestic market. In 2010, China overtook Japan as the second largest market in the world. To date, China is the world largest market for motor vehicles, with yearly sales of about 30 million units. Taking advantage of the growing demand by hundreds of millions of middle-income households, more and more export-oriented FIEs have increased local sales. For example, in the transportation equipment sector, Japanese-affiliated manufacturers in China exported about 84 of their products in 1996 — but by 2018, they sold virtually all of their products in the Chinese market.

Even more impressive is the role of FDI in the processing trade. Figure 6.1 presents the contribution of FIEs to processing exports. In 1995, FIEs accounted for 57 percent of processing exports. In subsequent years the dominance of FIEs in the processing trade grew steadily stronger; by 2008, FIEs were manufacturing almost 85 percent of processing exports. That percentage changed very little in the following decade. As explained previously, processing

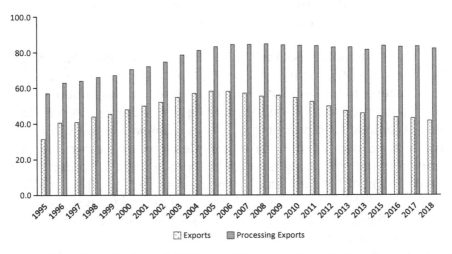

Figure 6.1 Contribution of FIEs to Chinese total exports and processing exports (Percentage)

Source: The author's calculations, based on Chinese Customs Office data.

exports are a component of GVCs and can be used as a direct measure of China's participation in GVCs. FDI is a major support for MNCs' offshoring of assembly and other tasks: the massive involvement of FDI in the Chinese processing trade is clear evidence that inflows of FDI have greatly facilitated China's integration into value chains of the global manufacturing industry.

China's accession to the WTO

Without any doubt, the processing trade regime has established a free trade environment in which imported materials and intermediate goods can enter China freely and Chinese assembled/made products can leave the country relatively unhindered. This special arrangement has definitely reduced the transaction costs of materials and goods moving in and out of China. On the other hand, the openness of foreign markets to Chinese goods has also shaped MNCs' willingness to offshore their production facilities to China and outsource goods and services from there. Chinese firms' involvement in GVCs requires that Chinese made/assembled products have an easy entry to international markets, with no more regulatory discrimination than that attached to goods from other nations. Bilateral and multilateral trade agreements guaranteeing Chinese goods access to foreign markets under favorable conditions are crucial to the participation of Chinese firms in GVCs. China has signed numerous bilateral and multilateral free trade agreements with its trading partners, and China's accession to the WTO in December 2001 was a catalyst that not only has broadened the scope of China's GVC participation, but also deepened China's involvement in value chains across almost all manufacturing sectors.

China's accession to the WTO has dramatically increased market access of Chinese goods to international markets. China has been granted permanent most-favored-nation (MFN) status by other WTO members, which has normalized China's trade relations with the rest of the world. This enhanced access to foreign markets has boosted China's exports in virtually all sectors (Wakasugi and Zhang, 2015). The WTO's dispute resolution mechanism also offers members some protection against discriminatory measures. Upon China's official entry to the WTO, several trading partners withdrew many of their restrictions on imports from China.

Before China entered the WTO in December 2001, China's trade with its partners had been regulated by a network of bilateral MFN agreements. The US and Europe had granted China MFN status soon after it launched its economic reforms; this opened the two largest foreign markets to Chinese goods. However, under the US Trade Act of 1974, China is classified as a non-market economy and could only be granted MFN status under certain conditions, notably the status had to be renewed annually. Without renewal, Chinese goods would be subject to the higher non-MFN tariff rates assigned to non-market economies by the Smoot–Hawley Tariff Act of 1930. The annual review requirement had given China's critics in the US Congress an opportunity to challenge the decision and left open the possibility that China's favorable access to the US market could be revoked; this insecurity deterred MNCs' reliance on Chinese goods for the US market. After the 1989 Tiananmen Square incident, an alliance of economic nationalists and human-rights groups attempted to deny China MFN status. In fact, the US House of Representatives had attempted to revoke China's temporary MFN status every year from 1990 to 2001, undermining the certainty of Chinese MFN status, and questioning the access of Chinese goods to the largest market in the world (Salam, 2020). Uncertainty over China's MFN status had definitely deterred offshoring and outsourcing to China by foreign MNCs, who had intended to take advantage of China's huge pool of cheap labor to serve the US market.

As part of the WTO entry negotiation process, the US Congress made the fateful decision to extend "permanent normal trade relations" (PNTR) to China in 2000. PNTR is a term used in US trade law, equivalent to the MFN status (Lardy, 2000). China's permanent accession to the WTO has eliminated the uncertainty associated with its MFN status, and encouraged US firms to open plants in China and outsource the production of cheap products to suppliers there (Pierce and Schott, 2016). At that time, the US was the most important export market for Japan, Korea and Taiwan. Companies from those economies, who had been targeting the US market, also took advantage of China's entry into the WTO and accelerated their offshoring to China, thus bolstering the involvement of the Chinese economy in GVCs.

Moreover, the WTO entry has enabled China to benefit from the organization's trade liberalizations. Exports of textiles and clothing from developing countries had been restricted under the Multifiber Arrangement. In 1995, the Uruguay Round Agreement on Textiles and Clothing (ATC) was approved by WTO members, formalizing their decision to phase out quotas on textiles and clothing exports from developing countries by 2005. As a consequence of its WTO accession, China has been included in the ATC and thus gained unrestricted access to the global market for textiles and clothing, both labor-intensive goods suitable to China's comparative advantage. With China's formal inclusion in the ATC, the abolition of quotas allowed China to make great use of its comparative advantage and expand its textiles and clothing exports worldwide (Brambilla *et al.*, 2009). The abolition of the Multifiber Arrangement has been crucial for hundreds of thousands of Chinese firms, who have become designated suppliers of global fashion vendors and large retailers such as H&M, ZARA, GAP and Walmart. The nullification of the Multifiber Arrangement radically accelerated the growth of Chinese textile and cloth exports. In the first four months of 2005, China's textile exports to EU countries surged 82 percent over the previous year; its textile and apparel exports to the US in April–May of 2005 were 66 percent greater than a year earlier. To control the sudden surge of Chinese textiles and apparel in both the US and EU markets, the Chinese government voluntarily agreed to limit the annual growth in that sector to 8–12.5 percent (Edmonds *et al.*, 2006).

The WTO accession further stimulated FDI into China, in particular export-oriented FDI in the manufacturing industry. While global FDI registered a decrease every year from 2001 to 2003, FDI into China experienced positive growth every year, with a sharp jump of 15 percent in 2001. In 2004, global FDI resumed growing, rising 2 percent that year; China observed a 13 percent increase in inflows of FDI. Before China's accession to the WTO, less than 60 percent of FDI went to the manufacturing sector; in the post-accession era, 70 percent (Whalley and Xin, 2010). That increase in FDI boosted the growth of processing exports and pushed the share of processing exports in China's total exports to 57 percent in 2006. It also strengthened the dominance of FIEs in the processing trade. China's involvement in GVCs was further enhanced by WTO-induced FDI inflows.

The ongoing US–China trade provides counterfactual evidence that the WTO entry was essential for China's successful participation in GCVs. Imposing a 25 percent tariff on $250 billion in Chinese goods, a unilateral action of the Trump administration, definitely violates the WTO's MFN rule. The tariff has made it more costly to source Chinese products for eventual exporting to the US market, and thus has prompted many firms to diversify their supply chains away from China. More than 80 percent of the fashion brands surveyed by the US Fashion Industry Association reported that they planned to reduce sourcing from China. Levi's reduced the share of its manufacturing in China from 16 percent in 2017 to less than 2 percent in 2019 (Kapadia, 2020).

Conclusion

In addition to China's intrinsic advantages, notably abundant cheap labor and close proximity to production networks developed by Japan and the Four Asian Tigers, policies implemented by the Chinese government to promote exports and FDI inflows contributed significantly to the success of China's participation in GVCs. These policies have nurtured a supportive environment which have not only encouraged MNCs to incorporate China in their value chains but also opened a window of opportunity for Chinese firms to get involved in value chains as designated suppliers or assemblers. The processing trade, FDI and accession to the WTO were the three most significant elements of policy initiatives that led to China's transformation into the center of global manufacturing value chains.

Before China joined the WTO, the Chinese government had imposed a variety of tariff and non-tariff barriers to restrict imports. However, it also instituted a processing trade regime to create a free trade environment for the import of materials and parts used for manufacturing exports. This was a revolutionary mechanism; it perfectly matched the needs of GVC lead firms in terms of assigning assembly and other low value-added tasks to Chinese firms in the service of international markets; and opened a gate to Chinese involvement in value chains immediately after the launch of the historic economic reforms. It is true that processing trade is present in many developing countries, but China is unequalled in terms of the scale of its processing trade and the scope of sectors covered. Almost all manufacturing sectors in China have been open to processing trade. At the peak, processing exports made up 57 percent of Chinese exports; even as recently as 2018, that share still exceeded one-third. The processing trade regime has been one of the most effective experiments toward China's participation in GVCs.

The offshoring of production activities is generally accompanied by greenfield investment abroad — one of the channels by which MNCs expand their value chains globally. China, which has aggressively promoted inflows of FDI since the early 1980s, particularly favored export-oriented FDI. The preferential tax policies and incentives provided by both the central and local governments made China the most popular recipient of FDI among developing countries. FIEs have dominated China's processing exports, with a share of more than 80 percent. They also accounted for more than half of Chinese exports during the period 2001–2010. This deep involvement of FIEs in Chinese exports reflects the importance of FDI in the facilitation of China's integration into GVCs.

The processing trade regime and FDI policy targeting China's internal environment have eliminated obstacles to the extension of GVCs into China. At the same time, China's accession to the WTO has dramatically expanded the access of Chinese products to the world market and secured China's MFN status. As an official member of the WTO, China has enjoyed the benefits of the organization's trade liberalization policies. The abolition of the Multifiber

Arrangement benefited China most and removed an obstacle to China's becoming the major supplier for global apparel vendors and large retailers. In other words, the WTO entry has improved China's external environment, creating the conditions necessary for the integration of China into value chains.

China's deep involvement in GVCs has also been supported by the Chinese policies aimed at logistic performance, intellectual property protection, and the development of transportation and telecommunications infrastructure. In the last several decades, China has spent more than 5 percent of its gross domestic product (GDP) on infrastructure investment, providing the transportation networks necessary for connecting both domestic suppliers and upstream foreign firms to overseas destination markets (Luo and Xu, 2018). Along with these policy elements, China's FDI policy, its processing trade regime and its WTO accession were the dominant factors underpinning China's transformation into the center of global manufacturing value chains.

Chapter 7

The Chinese Mobile Phone Industry and Its GVC Strategy

A typical value chain consists of a wide range of tasks requiring a variety of skills, ranging from labor intensive to capital intensive, and from information intensive to knowledge intensive. Lead firms of GVCs generally distribute each necessary task according to firm and national competitiveness in the required skills and resources. Apple CEO Tim Cook said, "The way that we do manufacturing is we look at all countries and look to see what skills are resident in each country, and we pick the best" (Murayama and Regalado, 2019).

To plug into GVCs successfully, a firm needs to identify tasks that match its specialties and areas of comparative advantage. Abundant cheap labor was China's comparative advantage at the beginning of its economic reforms. Initially, Chinese firms for the most part took advantage of China's cheap labor to gain entry into global value chains (GVCs), specializing in labor-intensive tasks such as assembly, the manufacturing of standard and low-skilled parts, and the supply of basic materials. This is true for Chinese firms in both labor-intensive and technology-intensive industries. Stitching Nike shoes, sewing UNIQLO jeans, making high-quality Paperblanks notebooks with imported materials, and assembling iPhones are examples of low-value added tasks performed by

Chinese firms in value chains managed by foreign multinational corporations (MNCs).

Specializing in low value-added tasks opens a door for Chinese firms to integrate themselves into GVCs. It is the beginning of the long march from entry into GVCs to participation in higher value-added segments, to capturing more value added, and ultimately evolving into a GVC lead firm. That evolutionary process is crucial for China to leverage value-chain participation so as to raise its income level and achieve full industrialization. It is relatively easy to enter low-skilled and low value-added segments of value chains, since the skills, training and investment required are limited, and the task thresholds are low. On the other hand, since entry is easy, many firms tend to maneuver for entry into low value-added segments of GVCs. Eager to benefit from the spillover effects of GVCs and implement value chain strategy for industrialization, more and more developing countries are jostling to enter those low value-added tasks, which intensifies the competition and erodes the benefits.

Cheap labor-based competition is not sustainable in the long run. To distinguish themselves from their rivals, firms absolutely must innovate their products and service offerings in order to move up along value chains and secure contracts for high value-added work. Otherwise, they risk falling into the so-called low value-added traps (Sturgeon and Kawakami, 2010). A few developing countries have been struggling with the middle-income trap, despite the fact that their industries have been integrated into GVCs. For example, Malaysia has been caught in the middle-income trap since the mid-1990s, largely because of failure to upgrade industrially. The Malaysian electronics industry, a pillar of the country's manufacturing industry, was integrated into GVCs in the early 1990s by the top five global contract manufacturers, Flex, Jabil Circuit, Celestica, Sanmina-SCI and Foxconn. These firms deployed their Malaysian subsidiaries in the labor-intensive assembly and testing of semiconductors, computer components and computers. Low worker-skill levels and government policy favoring an influx of low-wage foreign workers are the root causes of the Malaysian electronics industry being mired in low value-added tasks for some 30 years (Raj-Reichert, 2019).

As the global center of ICT assembly, China has become the world's top exporter of laptop computers, digital cameras and mobile phones. At the outset, some observers were not optimistic about China's value chain strategy, voicing the expectation that by adopting value chain strategy, Chinese mobile phone makers would "be more akin to Dell (which does little product research and design) than Tom Watson's IBM (which was highly vertically-integrated)" (Brandt and Thun, 2011). To date, the assembly of ICT products for foreign manufactures remains a main task of many Chinese firms. However, the development of the Chinese ICT industry in the last two decades shows that Chinese firms are not trapped in the so-called low value-added segments: many have moved to more sophisticated tasks and have captured more and more value added within GVCs led by foreign MNCs. Even more remarkably, a few Chinese firms have emerged as GVC lead firms with their own home-grown brands. In the global market for personal computers (PCs), the Chinese company Lenovo surpassed HP and Dell and ranked No. 1, with 24 percent of the global market in the 3rd quarter of 2019 (IDC, 2019). Similarly, in the global mobile phone market, home-grown Chinese brands Huawei, OPPO and Xiaomi are now three of the top five global smartphone brands (Counterpoint, 2019). The unprecedented success of the Chinese mobile phone industry is a classic story of success through GVC participation. In this chapter, I examine the case of the Chinese mobile phone industry to elucidate the mechanism by which GVCs helped Chinese firms enter the industry, penetrate international markets, achieve technology innovations and nurture indigenous brands.

The Chinese mobile phone industry: From assembly tasks upward

A typical mobile phone consists of 1,000–1,500 parts and components. Mobile phones are small enough to be handheld, which implies that some of their parts are so tiny that only human hands, not robots, can handle and assemble them into ready-to-use phones. As a result, assembly of mobile phones is very labor intensive. China's abundant cheap labor gave Chinese firms comparative advantage in performing that tedious and labor-intensive work. Initially, by specializing in the assembly Chinese firms took part in the value chains of global mobile phone makers; this enabled them to enter the industry and tap the explosive growth of global demand for mobile communications devices. At the outset, before the emergence of smartphones, China had been the assembly center for the world's major mobile phone brands, including Motorola and Nokia. Then, from the launch of the first generation iPhone onward, China had been the exclusive assembler of iPhones.

At its peak, Samsung, the leading mobile phone maker in the world, had 65 percent of its mobile phones assembled in China. The outsourcing activities of global mobile phone manufacturers have transformed China into the largest mobile phone exporter in the world, despite its technological deficiencies in the manufacture of core components and the design of operating systems. This trend has continued. Rising demand for mobile phones and constant technological innovation by international makers have been driving the explosive growth of Chinese mobile phone production and exports.

To illustrate the contribution of GVCs to the development of the Chinese mobile phone industry and the importance of assembly as an entry point for Chinese firms to benefit from the newly emerged high-technology market, I examine the growth of Chinese mobile phone outputs and exports during the period 2000–2012. There are three reasons for doing so. First, that was the period when both outputs and exports of Chinese mobiles experienced exponential growth. Second, during this period, most mobile phones made in China were actually destined for foreign markets rather than the domestic market. Last, and most important, the presence of indigenous Chinese brands on international markets was negligible. Indigenous Chinese brand mobile phones contributed very little to the expansion of China's mobile phone exports during that growth period, so I can ignore the impact of indigenous Chinese brands.

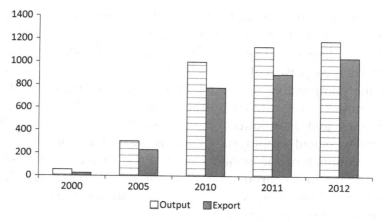

Figure 7.1 Chinese mobile phone outputs and exports (Million units), 2000–2012
Sources: UNCOMTRDE and China Statistics Bureau.

Figure 7.1 shows Chinese mobile phone production and exports from 2000 to 2012. As can be seen in the figure, at the beginning of the 21st century the scale of China's mobile phone production and exports was relatively small. In 2000, China produced 52.5 million mobile handsets, of which 22.8 million, or about 43 percent of the total, were exported to overseas markets. During this period, mobile phones gradually replaced personal computers as integrated devices for instant communication, games, entertainment and photos. The trend has accelerated with the advent of smartphones. Driven by the explosive growth in global demand and the rapid technology innovation in the mobile phone sector, China's annual output of mobile phones expanded almost 20-fold, surging to 998.3 million units by 2010. Exports grew even faster, skyrocketing to 776 million that year; China became the leading exporter in the world. In 2012, China's annual mobile phone export volume reached a milestone of one billion mark. It is important to emphasize that, between 2005 and 2012, China's mobile phone exports consistently accounted for more than three quarters of annual national output. At the peak in 2012, China shipped 1.03 billion mobile phones abroad, more than 87 percent of China's output for the year.

Given that all made in China mobile phones during the period were made with core technology components (CPU, NAND and DRAM) and operating systems from foreign companies, clearly the unprecedented growth of Chinese mobile phone exports had little to with the comparative advantage and competitiveness of Chinese firms: rather it was driven by the spillover effects of the brands, technology and distribution networks of the global mobile phone makers who had employed China as their assembly base. The export volumes of the period clearly attest to the crucial role of value chains in the promotion of exports of "made/assembled in China" mobile phones. Not only did the innovation and marketing activities of the lead firms (Motorola, Nokia, Apple and Samsung) stimulate global demand for mobile phones but they also increased demand for the low-skilled and low value-added services of Chinese workers.

Upgrading along the iPhone value chain

Plugging into a GVC is similar to engaging in a dynamic learning curve, in that it enables non-lead firms to innovate and upgrade. Firms that embrace the learning opportunities offered by GVC participation can significantly enhance their innovation and upgrade their contribution to value chains. In any value chain, the lead firm defines the products, sets the quality standards and specifies the technical parameters. All non-lead firms are obliged to follow the design rules set by the lead firm. Intensive communication and information exchange between the lead firm and the suppliers are common; this affords a unique channel by which non-lead firms can access new knowledge and production know-how. For instance, The transformation of some Asian apparel industry suppliers from original equipment manufacturers (OEMs) to original design manufacturers (ODMs) was largely the result of their participation in apparel commodity chains (Gereffi, 1999).

For low-level entrants to GVCs, the learning opportunities within GVCs include face-to-face interaction, knowledge transfer from lead firms, pressure to adopt international standards, and training of the local workforce by lead firms (Marchi *et al.*, 2017). This learning facilitates industrial upgrading and innovation activities of GVC non-lead firms, such as adding value to products; moving up from pure assembly to design work; and increasing production process efficiency (Morrison *et al.*, 2008).

Chinese mobile phone firms have been following two distinctive upgrading trajectories, linear and nonlinear. Linear upgrading basically moves along a value chain step by step, from low value-added tasks to high value-added ones. For instance, a firm might start assembling mobile phones; then enters the manufacture of low skilled and non-core components; gradually develops the technology capacity required for the production of core parts such as memory chips and CPUs; and eventually designs mobile phones with its own brand. Linear innovation differs from the conventional linear model of a process starting with basic research and eventually moving on to stages such as applied research, development and diffusion (Godin, 2006). Xiaomi's MIU interface, OPPO's VOOC flash charging technology, and Huawei's Kirin processor are examples of linear innovation and upgrading along value chains. Whereas sourcing core technology from foreign suppliers and jumping directly to brand building leads to a nonlinear model of innovation. Chinese original brand manufacturers (OBMs) have adopted the nonlinear model by taking advantage of the modularization of mobile phone production and have successfully broken the monopoly of foreign rivals in both domestic and international markets.

When Apple launched its first generation iPhone, only Foxconn was involved in the production of the iPhone, assembling parts supplied by American, Japanese, Korean and German companies into ready-to-use iPhones (in a Foxconn factory in Shenzhen China). The assembly fee $6.5 per iPhone 3G was the entire value added contributed by China to the manufacture of the iPhone 3G; it was the smallest contribution among all the countries involved in the iPhone value chain. The emergence of the iPhone and its dominance of the smartphone market have offered the Chinese mobile phone industry an excellent opportunity to grow and benefit from the rising demand for smartphones. As the center for iPhone assembly, the

Chinese mobile phone industry has benefited significantly from the popularity of the iPhone in the world market. The constantly rising demand for the iPhone in the world market has always translated automatically into demand for the services and peripheral components supplied by the Chinese mobile phone industry. By 2018, Apple had sold roughly 1.6 billion iPhones since the rollout of the first generation iPhone, a significant contribution to the growth of the Chinese mobile phone industry in recent decades.

In 2018, Apple rolled out the iPhone X, the 12th generation iPhone. With the introduction of the iPhone X, which carries the most advanced technologies, including 3D sensing technology, we see more and more Chinese companies participating in iPhone value chains at higher levels, performing more sophisticated technological tasks and contributing more value added. Those successful upgrades demonstrate that Chinese firms are not trapped in the low value-added segment of the manufacture of the iPhone.

Becoming a designated Apple supplier or moving into relatively high value-added segments of iPhone production is extremely rewarding financially. Once a Chinese firm joins an array of Apple supply companies, hundreds of millions of Apple users around the world are potential customers for that firm's products or services. That predictable and lucrative prospect motivates Chinese firms to raise the quality of their products to meet the standards of Apple, and thus qualify as an Apple supplier. The supplier list published by Apple reveals that Chinese firms have strengthened their presence and played increasingly important roles in the value chains controlled by Apple. In 2014, of 198 companies in Apple's supply chains, 14 were Chinese, a few of them supplying core components such as displays and printed circuit boards (Grimes and Sun, 2016).

Table 7.1 lists Chinese firms and their allotted tasks in the production of the iPhone 3G and the iPhone X. In the case of the iPhone 3G, Foxconn was the only firm located in China, performing the task with least value added: assembly. In the case of the iPhone X, besides Foxconn, there are 10 local Chinese firms involved, supplying non-core components and performing tasks beyond simple assembly, spread over relatively sophisticated segments.

Table 7.1   iPhone 3G and iPhone X tasks performed in China

3G iPhone (2009)	iPhone X (2018)
• Assembly (Foxconn)	• Assembly (Foxconn);
	• Function parts for touchscreen module (Anjie Technology);
	• Filter for 3D sensing module (Crystal Optech);
	• Coil module for wireless charging (Lushare Precision);
	• Printed circuit board (M-Flex);
	• Speakers (Goertek);
	• RF antenna (Shenzhen Sunway);
	• Battery pack (Sunwoda);
	• Glass cover (Lens Technology);
	• Stainless frame (Kersen Technology);
	• Camera module (O-Filem).

Source: Xing (2020a).

For example, Sunwoda, a leading Chinese battery maker, supplies the iPhone battery pack. Sony batteries were used in the early models of the iPhone; Sunwoda's supplanting of Sony as a battery pack supplier is a significant move up the iPhone value chain. Kersen Technology provides the stainless frames, and Lens Technology manufactures the glass covers. In addition, Chinese companies Anjie Technology and Lushare Precision are involved in manufacturing iPhone X touch screens and 3D sensing modules, respectively. Touch screens and 3D sensing modules are critical technological components of the iPhone X. The former translate the user's finger movements into data that can be interpreted as commands, while the latter are a key element of the facial recognition system, a feature introduced in the iPhone X. Chinese company Dongshan Precision has joined the suppliers of Apple by acquiring American company M-Flex. Chinese companies Goertech, Shenzhen Sunway, Crystal-Optech and O-film provide functional parts: speakers, RF antennas, filters and camera modules, respectively.

The involvement of those Chinese firms, even though in non-core technology segments of the Phone X value chain, indicates that the Chinese mobile phone industry as a whole has moved to the upper rungs of the iPhone value chain ladder. It is worthy of mention that all core components embedded in the printed circuit board assembly (PCBA) of the iPhone X, including the processor, DRAM, NAND, display and camera, are supplied by non-Chinese companies including Apple, Qualcomm, Broadcom, Samsung, Toshiba and Sony. These core components constitute a road map for future upgrading and technological innovation by the Chinese mobile phone industry.

For estimation of the domestic value added in a country's exports, and for fair evaluation of bilateral trade balances between a country and its trading partners, it is appropriate to use the manufacturing cost of a product as a benchmark. To determine the value captured by Chinese firms in the whole iPhone X value chain, we should use the retail price rather than the production cost as a benchmark, since the retail price proxies for total value added of the iPhone X. Figure 7.2 compares the Chinese value added in the iPhone X with that in the iPhone 3G. In terms of production costs, China captured a mere 3.6 percent of the value added of the iPhone 3G, while its share of the iPhone X was 25.4 percent, a remarkable increase over the period 2009–2018. Taking retail price as a benchmark, we see that China received 10.4 percent for each iPhone X sold at $1,000, much higher than the 1.3 percent for each iPhone 3G

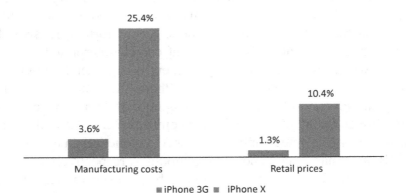

Figure 7.2   Chinese value added embedded in the iPhone 3G and iPhone X

Source: Xing (2020a).

sold at $500. The sale of 217 million iPhones in the global market in 2018, along with the successful upward movement of Chinese firms along the iPhone value chain, brought huge economic benefit to China. Ferguson and Schularick (2009) coined the term "Chimerica" to describe the close economic cooperation between China and the US. The iPhone is a typical micro example of Chimerica. Thanks to China's involvement in Apple value chains, the success of Apple in innovation and marketing has always brought huge benefits to the Chinese economy.

The rise of Chinese home-grown global brands

Chinese firms' upward movement along the iPhone value chain, to the manufacture of relatively sophisticated parts and the performance of tasks beyond assembly, is a case of linear upgrading along GVCs. In addition to manufacturing handsets for foreign OBMs, the Chinese mobile phone industry has created a few mobile phone brands which are competitive with foreign brands in both China and abroad. Huawei, Xiaomi OPPO and Vivo, the best known Chinese mobile phone brands, have eroded the market share of their foreign rivals and have completely eliminated foreign domination of the sector in the Chinese market. The emergence of the Chinese brands is a result of the nonlinear upgrading path.

Huawei, once the largest mobile phone maker in China and the second largest in the world, is regarded as the most innovative Chinese company. In 2018, it invested $15.3 billion in R&D, outspending even Apple (Bloomberg, 2019a). Huawei's innovations are more technology-oriented than those of other Chinese mobile phone manufacturers. Huawei has developed the Kirin processor, which is used in its latest model, the Huawei P30 Pro. According to the teardown data of the Japanese firm Fomalhaut Techno Solution (Tanaka, 2019), the Huawei P30 Pro is powered by a Kirin processor made by HiSilicon, a subsidiary of Huawei; this suggests that Huawei has developed the technological capacity to produce a replacement for Qualcomm chipsets, which are currently used by most Chinese mobile phone makers. The Kirin processor marks the highest level of technological innovation by the Chinese mobile phone industry to date.

OPPO, marketing its phone as a camera phone, ranked No. 3 in the Chinese market after Huawei and Vivo, with a 16 percent share in Q4 of 2019 (Counterpoint, 2020a). Thanks to their excellent selfie experience, OPPO smartphones have achieved widespread popularity among young people. OPPO actually styles its phones as camera phones in commercials so as to differentiate OPPO from other brands. The company operates a nationwide network of 200,000 stores selling its products in China; to motivate its sales personnel, it generally pays a much more generous commission than the industrial average (Wang, 2016).

On the back of every OPPO phone is a line of text, "Designed by OPPO Assembled in China" — an imitation of the original phrase on the back of the iPhone. It has a strange ring to it, since OPPO is clearly a 100 percent Chinese company. OPPO's use of the slogan is a message to its users: OPPO phones are made of the state-of-the-art technologies, but China's role is limited to assembly — which is self-evident in that OPPO phones are products of GVCs.

In Q4 of 2019, Xiaomi was the fifth largest mobile phone maker in China, according to the shipment data. Different from OPPO, Xiaomi is a factoryless maker — it has no assembly facilities. It outsources the production of its phones to contract manufacturers. Xiaomi is also the first Chinese mobile phone vendor to sell phones exclusively online. Xiaomi's largest foreign market is India, where it surpassed Samsung to become the No. 1 smartphone vendor in 2018.

Marketing research by Counterpoint (2020a) shows that in Q4 of 2019, Chinese brands captured 86 percent of the Chinese smartphone market, led by Huawei with 35 percent. The top three smartphone brands in terms of shipments (Huawei, Vivo, OPPO) were all Chinese brands; together they account for 68 percent of the Chinese market, while Apple retaining a mere 14 percent of the Chinese market. The share of Samsung, the No. 1 mobile phone maker in the world, shrank to zero in 2019 (Figure 7.3). Things had been so different back in 2012: Samsung was then the largest vendor in the Chinese market, with 14 percent market share, while Huawei had

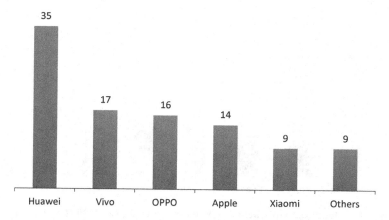

Figure 7.3   Chinese smartphone market share by brand, Q4 2019 (Percentage)
Source: Counterpoint (2020a).

only 10 percent, and the market shares of OPPO, Vivo and Xiaomi were negligible (Chen and Wen, 2013).

Similarly, the global mobile phone market had been virtually dominated by Samsung, Apple and other foreign brands until 2012. For instance, Samsung, the largest, captured 39.6 percent of the global market in 2012, while Apple, the second largest mobile phone maker, accounted for 25.1 percent; Blackberry, Nokia and HTC together had 18.4 percent. Only 16.9 percent of market share belonged to other brands, including Sony, Huawei and Motorola (Chen and Wen, 2013). Riding on their success in the home market, Chinese OBMs started selling mobile phones with their own brands in the global market. Mobile phones marketed under Chinese brands have gradually increased their presence and market shares in geographically dispersed foreign markets. A few Chinese brands have emerged as well-known global brands, especially in emerging markets, where low-income population are a ready market for Chinese brand mobile phones, which are generally cheaper than high-end phones like iPhones. For instance, Chinese phone makers including Xiaomi, OPPO, Vivo and Realme held 68 percent of India's smartphone market in Q4 2019. Xiaomi has been the most successful Chinese brand in India; it has surpassed Samsung and become the country's most popular smartphone brand, with

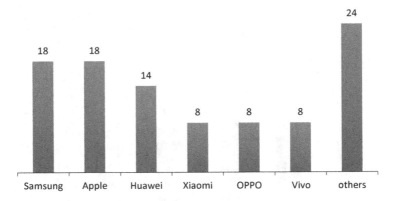

Figure 7.4   Global smartphone market share by brand, Q4 2019 (Percentage)
Source: Counterpoint (2020b).

27 percent market share (Candytech, 2020). The relatively low prices of Chinese brand phones are very attractive to low income consumers, who are the majority of mobile phone users in India.

In Q4 of 2019, Huawei ranked third, with a global market share of 14 percent, just 4 percent points less than that of Samsung. OPPO, Vivo and Xiaomi each accounted for 8 percent of the global market share in that quarter (Figure 7.4). In fact, OPPO and Vivo belong to the same company, BBK Electronics Corporation, a Chinese multinational firm specializing in electronics. The combined market share of OPPO and Vivo at that time was 16 percent. In other words, BBK Electronics Corporation was actually the third largest mobile phone maker in the world.

Sourcing foreign technology to foster home-grown brands

To a large extent, the expansion of GVCs in the mobile phone industry can be attributed to the rise of modularity, i.e., the breaking down of the manufacture of complicated products into modules — sub-systems that can be designed and manufactured independently. Modularity allows firms to mix and match components to produce final products tailored to various consumer preferences. By leveraging modularity in their product design, firms can improve their product innovation rate (Baldwin and Clark, 1997). The modularization of mobile phone production has reduced production complexity and allowed potential market entrants to concentrate on non-core technology activities such as assembly and brand development. The modularization of mobile phone production substantially lowers entry barriers, so firms from developing countries can easily enter the industry by sourcing technology components so as to overcome their disadvantages in operating systems and semiconductor fabrication. Chinese home-grown brands Huawei, Xiaomi, OPPO and Vivo have emerged as a result of those firms' adoption of GVC strategy. Despite their relatively limited technology capacity to produce core components such as processors and memory chips, Chinese mobile phone makers have been able to enter the mobile phone industry by sourcing core technological components from foreign MNCs and focusing on incremental innovation, marketing and brand building.

At the early stage of mobile phone development, the production of mobile phones was a complicated process, vertically integrated within a single firm. In that setting, a few large firms in industrialized countries (e.g., Nokia, Ericsson and Texas Instruments) monopolized global markets. In 2001, Wavecom, the French firm that first introduced the GSM model, developed the first modular design, which allowed handset makers to easily integrate applications into one main board. Taking advantage of that modularization, China's TCL, an electronic appliance maker, entered the mobile phone market in 2004 (Sun *et al.*, 2010).

In 2006, MediaTek (MTK), a fabless Taiwanese semiconductor firm, developed a turnkey solution: an integrated solution combining hardware and software on a single chip that combines a baseband platform and multimedia (sound and image) data processor. That solution was a milestone in the development of the Chinese mobile phone industry; it greatly enhanced the degree of modularity of mobile phone production, which was especially valuable for small phone makers who lacked the requisite technology capacity.

Using the chip, firms could easily modify product functionality to cater to the preferences of diverse consumers; entry barriers were lowered significantly. MTK's turnkey solution prompted the proliferation of *shanzhai* mobile phone makers (*shanzhai* originally meaning counterfeit or imitation products), who had previously served as either OEMs or distributors for leading mobile phone brands. However, a few studies argued that *shanzhai* phones were indigenous innovation products by small phone makers, and that they were good enough products with affordable prices that met the needs of the targeted customers. *Shanzhai* phone makers gained market share not through technology innovation, but by adopting a novel business model (Hu *et al.*, 2011).

In the age of smartphones, the Android operating system (OS) and Qualcomm processor chipsets have become standard technology platforms. As of 2018, leading Chinese smart phone makers ZTE, Xiaomi, OPPO and Vivo have all adopted the Android OS for use in their smartphones; Xiaomi and OPPO built 70 percent of their phones on Qualcomm platforms; ZTE and Vivo used Qualcomm platforms for 60 percent and 50 percent of their phones, respectively (World Bank, 2019). The Android OS platform has lowered technology barriers for handset assemblers who until now were only capable of manufacturing white-box phones; this has enabled a few Chinese OEMs to evolve into OBMs — OPPO being a noteworthy example (Chen and Wen, 2013).

Adopting foreign technology platforms and focusing on brand development and product differentiation is a strategy commonly adopted by Chinese firms to overcome their technological shortcomings. Platform adoption takes much less time and investment than developing core technology such as chipsets and operating systems. The risk involved in core technology development is very high: it is uncertain whether Chinese firms could develop the technology capacity to produce necessary core components, even with massive investment. Further, development of core technology requires specialized human resources that are in very short supply in China. Even if those firms could design an operating system or chipsets, it is unclear whether the OS and chipsets developed by Chinese firms could compete with the established technology of foreign firms. The modularization of the mobile phone industry makes it possible for latecomers to enter the industry using modules available from foreign firms. The huge Chinese market, a population of 1.4 billion, is conducive to marketing-focused strategies drawing on borrowed technology. In China, a focus on the domestic market reduces the marketing gap and encourages Chinese mobile phone makers to concentrate on marketing and product differentiation. Generally they have more information than leading foreign mobile phone makers about Chinese consumers, and a better understanding of them. At the early stages of their development, Chinese mobile phone makers for the most part adopted a low price strategy to attract consumers who could not afford expensive foreign brands, and target consumers in the country's third and fourth tier cities, which had not attracted much attention from foreign brand vendors. In addition, the Chinese makers explored niche markets, introducing a variety of peripherals such as dual SIM cards, selfie specialization and long life batteries (Brandt and Thun, 2011).

To elucidate the dependence of Chinese brand mobile phones on foreign technology platforms, Table 7.2 lists the core components and operating systems used by three Chinese brand mobile phones: the Huawei P30 Pro, the Xiaomi MIX 2 and the OPPO R11s. All three models run on the Android operating system. The Huawei P30 Pro is powered by the Kirin processor. In addition, the Huawei

Table 7.2   Dependence of Chinese brand mobile phones on foreign technology

	Huawei P30 Pro	Xiaomi MIX 2	OPPO R11s
Operating system	Android (US)	Android (US)	Android (US)
CPU	HiSilicon (China)	Qualcomm (US)	Qualcomm (US)
NAND	Samsung (Korea)	Hynix (Korea)	Samsung (Korea)
DRAM	Micron Technology (US)	Samsung (Korea)	Samsung (Korea)
Display	BOE Technology (China)	JDI (Japan)	Samsung (Korea)

Source: Xing and He (2018) and Tanaka (2019).

P30 Pro incorporates an OLED display manufactured by China's BOE Technology. The OLED display is the most expensive part embedded in the Huawei P30 Pro. Because of those two key components, the Chinese value added in the Huawei P30 Pro is 38.1 percent. Samsung, LG and Japan Device Inc. (JDI) have until now been dominant in the OLED display market; Huawei's adoption of BOE Technology's OLED display is a noticeable encroachment on the monopoly of foreign companies. The Huawei P30 Pro uses DRAM from US firm Micron Technology and NAND from Samsung. All foreign parts and components together account for 61.9 percent of the production cost of the Huawei P30 Pro. Clearly, this is a GVC product, even though it is designed by the most innovative Chinese company, it is still significantly dependent on foreign technologies.

The OPPO R11s, a premium smartphone released in 2017, is another illuminating case. It is powered by Qualcomm's Snapdragon 660 mid-range processor, coupled with an embedded multi-chip package (eMCP) by Samsung. It features a 6.1-inch full screen AMOLED display by Samsung. All components embedded in the PCBA are supplied by foreign companies, particularly Qualcomm, Samsung, TDK and Muruta. The total value added of foreign companies accounts for 83.3 percent of the total manufacturing costs, consistent with the phrase "Designed by OPPO Assembled in China" printed on the back of OPPO phones.

Similar to OPPO smartphones, Xiaomi's flagship MIX 2, released in the second half of 2017, is powered by a top-end processor, Qualcomm Snapdragon 835. It has 6GB NAND flash memory supplied by the Korean company Hynix, and 64GB DRAM manufactured by Samsung. It features a 5.99 inch 1080 × 2160 pixel display produced by JDI. In total, foreign companies account for 84.6 percent of the value added in the Xiaomi MIX 2, an extraordinarily high degree of reliance on sourced foreign technologies.

The content of Table 7.2 suggests that foreign technology is still indispensable for the manufacture of Chinese brand mobile phones, even those made by the most innovative Chinese company, Huawei.

In spite of the emergence of OPPO and Xiaomi as global brands, the significantly high foreign value added in their products (more than 80 percent of the bill of materials) shows that innovation by the two companies is incremental and marginal. Instead of targeting drastic technology advancement to catch up, these two famous smartphone vendors concentrate on product differentiation and brand building, taking advantage of available technology platforms. The success of OPPO and Xiaomi indicate that GVCs provide a nonlinear model of innovation, and that by sourcing necessary technologies, Chinese firms can enter high-technology industry and emerge as lead firms.

Innovation is not confined to technology improvement; brand development is also an important form of innovation. In the age of GVCs, sourcing technology is a new business model, as seen in the success of Chinese mobile phone vendors Huawei, Xiaomi and OPPO. Brands give firms the power to control value chains and often constitute the largest value added of a lead firm's products. Using retail prices as a benchmark, the estimated domestic value added of the Xiaomi MIX2 is 41.7 percent, while the domestic value added of the OPPO R11s accounts for 45.3 percent of its retail price. Brand premium is one of the major factors raising the domestic value added in the two sample phones (Xing and He, 2018).

Conclusion

The unprecedented blossoming of the Chinese mobile phone industry is an impressive example of the successful adoption of GVC strategy. Even today, there is still a big technology gap between Chinese companies and foreign lead firms in the mobile phone industry. No Chinese company has developed an operating system, and Chinese brand mobile phones remain dependent on chipsets made by companies such as Qualcomm, Samsung, Hynix, and Micron Technology. Nevertheless, by adopting value chain strategy, China has become the world's largest maker and the largest exporter of mobile phones. Of the top five global mobile phone brands, three are Chinese: Huawei, Xiaomi and OPPO. Technology deficiencies have not blocked the emergence of the Chinese mobile phone industry. The value chain strategy of sourcing necessary technology platforms and concentrating on product differentiation and incremental innovation accounts for the substantial recent achievements of the Chinese mobile phone industry. GVCs facilitated by modularization have provided a unique path by which Chinese firms have entered the industry and jumped over technological hurdles. The emergence of Chinese home-grown brands in global markets and the upgrading of Chinese firms along the iPhone value chain show that Chinese firms are capable of moving to higher technological stages of value chain work, and that through innovation they can successfully compete with foreign rivals.

Being latecomers, Chinese firms had to enter value chains as contract manufacturers, assembling mobile phones for foreign vendors such as Apple — but they have not let themselves be trapped in low value-added segments. More and more Chinese firms have moved to the upper rungs of the iPhone value chain ladder by upgrading and innovating. Chinese firms captured a mere 3.6 percent of value added in the first generation iPhone — but their value-added contribution surged to 25.4 percent, $104, in the iPhone X. More than 1.6 billion iPhones had been sold on the global market; thanks to GVC strategy, Chinese firms have been involved in the iPhone value chain and benefited tremendously from the success of the American company Apple.

The development of GVCs makes it possible to pursue a nonlinear model of innovation, but GVC strategy is not risk-free. The GVC strategy of the Chinese mobile phone industry is based on an assumption that Chinese firms would be able to purchase necessary technologies via fair market transactions. The US blacklisting of Huawei has disrupted Huawei's supply chains; clearly, it is no longer viable for Huawei to source American technologies. If the US government extends its technology sanctions to include other Chinese mobile phone makers, the Chinese mobile phone industry will be in jeopardy. Given the uncertainty of China–US relations, it is imperative that Chinese mobile phone makers search for alternative suppliers or invest in indigenous technology, or both.

Chapter 8

Trade War and Pandemic: Dark Shadows over China-Centered GVCs

Like an invisible hand, global value chains (GVCs) have deeply integrated the Chinese economy into the global economy. The scope and scale of Chinese firms' involvement in GVCs have led to the appearance of China-centered GVCs in global manufacturing. As Chinese firms have gradually improved their technology capacities, they have moved beyond simple assembly and moved up GVC chains into relatively high value-added tasks, providing parts and components to upstream foreign firms. At the time of writing, China was the world's largest exporter of motor vehicle parts and accessories and the largest supplier of active pharmaceutical ingredients (APIs) to global pharmaceutical companies. The dominance in international markets of Chinese-made textiles, clothing, telecommunications equipment and office and electronic data processing machines, and China's refusal to allow itself to be trapped in low value-added segments, have further entrenched China's central position in GVCs for manufactured products. Even more impressive, by adopting GVC strategy, a few indigenous Chinese firms such as Lenovo, Huawei, OPPO and Xiaomi have emerged as lead firms and have built up their own GVCs, following a nonlinear upgrading path by concentrating on brand development and sourcing core technologies from foreign firms.

GVC strategy, however, is not risk free. As value chains are sliced ever thinner and dispersed over more countries, value chains have become more vulnerable to external shocks. An external shock to one segment (whether skill-intensive or not) of a value chain would quite likely disrupt the operations of the whole chain, affecting all the firms positioned along the chain. Natural disasters, geopolitical tensions and trade wars are all potential threats to the smooth operations and reliability of value chains. The unfolding US–China trade war and the COVID-19 pandemic have exposed the vulnerability of China-centered GVCs. The punitive tariffs imposed by the Trump administration on Chinese goods have substantially increased the costs of assembling goods in or sourcing products from China for the US market, while the shutdown of Chinese factories due to the outbreak of the COVID-19 suddenly not only disrupted the operations of upstream factories in various nations but also caused international market shortages of medical supplies desperately needed for fighting the pandemic, items such as sanitizers, ventilators and personal protective equipment. As the trade war evolves into a technological war, a few leading Chinese high-technology companies, which have been pursuing GVC strategy and have grown dependent on core technology modules of American companies, have been blacklisted by the US government. They have been deprived of the right to source American technologies. This has severely disrupted the operations of their supply chains and even put their survival in question.

The trade war has necessitated the redeployment of China-centered GVCs. GVC lead firms from the US, Japan and other countries have been shifting parts of their supply chains out of China, either back home or to third countries. The COVID-19 pandemic has further intensified that trend. The pandemic has been a lesson to all governments: from the perspective of national security, medical equipment and pharmaceutical products should be given the same importance as food and energy, and should be included in the list of goods essential for national security. Reshoring production of essential medical supplies, which may become a new trend in value chain restructuring, will further diminish the central position of Chinese firms in GVCs. US sanctions on Chinese technology firms such as Huawei have triggered the process of technology decoupling between the two largest economies, alerting China to tremendous risks inherent in sourcing core technologies from American companies for Chinese industrial development, and further reinforcing the determination of the Chinese government to be independent in core semiconductor technologies. Profit-maximization and efficiency improvement drove the development of GVCs over the last four decades. In the future, avoidance of geopolitical risks and preparation for natural disasters such as the COVID-19 pandemic will steer the trajectory of GVC operations. In this chapter, I analyze the impacts of the US–China trade war and the COVID-19 pandemic on the future trajectory of value chains and discuss possible scenarios.

First shock to China-centered GVCs: The US–China trade war

Free trade, or at least a low trade barrier environment, is a necessary condition for optimal allocation of value chain tasks across countries. Goods manufactured along GVCs usually cross national borders more than once. Trade barriers increase transaction costs in terms of customs clearance and documentation, while tariffs add extra costs for both intermediates and final goods. China's processing trade regime has effectively institutionalized a free trade environment, which has been conducive to Chinese firms' participation in value chains. The ongoing US–China trade war, however, has spoiled the environment necessary for China to function either as an assembler of or an outsourcing center for goods catering to the US market.

President Trump had repeatedly claimed that trade between China and the US is unfair, because US tariffs on Chinese products are much lower than those imposed by China on American goods. This asymmetric tariff structure has given an advantage to Chinese exports entering the US market, and hindered American products' access to the Chinese market. China's industrial policy and subsidies have also been alleged to be unfair trade practices, as they have given an edge to Chinese firms competing with American companies. Those unfair trade practices have been one of the major drivers of the growth of the US trade deficit with China. Moreover, the Trump administration had accused China of intellectual property theft and of forcing American companies to transfer their technology to their Chinese partners (White House, 2018). Given its rapid economic growth and gigantic size, China appears to be a viable challenger to the US dominance in the world economy. The skyrocketing US trade deficit with China and the ambitions of *Made in China 2025* reinforce US concerns about the threat of China's rising economic power. The Trump administration expected to use a trade war to rewrite the trade rules; to force China to further open its market to American firms; to abandon unfair practices that distort the competition between American and Chinese firms — all to enable the US to compete with China on a level playing field (Xing, 2018b).

President Trump had been using tariffs to wage a trade war with China. He believes that tariffs are the most powerful and effective weapon and can force the Chinese government to sign a trade deal on US terms. So far, the Trump administration levied a 25 percent tariff on $250 billion in Chinese goods, including electronics, furniture and machinery. One of the main reasons why GVC lead firms in ICT assigned assembly-the low skill and labor-intensive tasks to firms in China, is low labor cost. The low cost has also driven large global retailers to outsource to Chinese firms the production of low value products such as apparel, footwear, toys, and Christmas and birthday decorations. Regardless of whether Chinese firms or foreign buyers pay the 25 percent tariff, the tariff surely raises the cost of made in China goods destined for the US market, and erodes Chinese suppliers' cost advantage over other developing countries such as India, Indonesia and Vietnam.

In fact, the detrimental impact of the tariff is much larger than the rate suggests, because the tariff is imposed on gross value of Chinese goods, rather than the Chinese value added. Chinese exports generally contain a large portion of imported foreign intermediates. For example, the foreign value added in Chinese ICT exports to the US is estimated to have been 54 percent in 2014. The negative effect of the tariff is multiplied via value chains. Parts and components are made in third countries, e.g., Japan and Korea, but eventually they are used in products assembled in China, and so are also subject to the 25 percent tariff, which significantly raises the cost of products assembled in China. Taking the iPhone X as an example, a 25 percent tariff would increase the cost of an iPhone X assembled in China by $102, almost equal to the entire Chinese value added embedded in the phone. In other words, the nominal 25 percent tariff imposed on the gross value is in effect a 100 percent tariff on the Chinese value added.

The tariff burden, in combination with foreign value added, cannot be offset by conventional means such as productivity improvement, cost reduction or currency depreciation, since imported intermediates are exogenous to the operations of Chinese firms. It is almost impossible for foreign retailers to absorb the 25 percent tariff without suffering a huge loss of profits, so conventional approaches to circumventing punitive tariffs are not realistic. The only viable option would be shifting part of supply chains out of China. Many multinational corporations (MNCs) have begun reorganizing their GVCs, moving their factories out of China or searching for alternatives in third countries — and as a result reshaping China-centered GVCs geographically. Chinese contract manufacturers are facing the possibility of being replaced by suppliers in other countries. The reorganization of existing value chains unambiguously undercuts China's export capacity; this is even more damaging than the direct effect of the tariffs on costs.

In a value chain, Chinese suppliers are obliged to follow the lead firm. They mainly perform tasks in production stages, and passively comply with orders as to what to produce and how much. Their relations with lead firms are asymmetric and they have no say as to where their products are sold. That arrangement frees Chinese firms of the risks associated with R&D, brand development and marketing, which is one advantage of participation in GVCs. On the other hand, when lead firms decide to search for alternative suppliers or redeploy their supply chains in response to the trade war, Chinese firms face the danger of losing their GVC membership. Many buyer-driven GVCs rely on China as a source of low value and low-skilled products. It is relatively easy for lead firms of buyer-driven GVCs such as Walmart, UNIQLO and H&M to find alternative suppliers in other developing countries such as Vietnam, Bangladesh and Indonesia. Given the asymmetric power balance between lead firms and Chinese suppliers, Chinese firms have little leverage to influence the re-organization of value chains. If the re-organization trend persists long enough, China will find itself no longer playing a central role in the GVCs targeting the US market.

In a survey by the American Chamber of Commerce in China (2019), approximately 40 percent of the respondents reported that they were considering relocating, or had already relocated, their manufacturing facilities outside China. For those that planned to move their manufacturing out of China, the top destinations are Southeast Asia (24.7 percent) and Mexico (10.5 percent). The trade war also prompted Apple, which had virtually all its products assembled in China, to consider restructuring its China-centered value chains: Apple asked its major suppliers to evaluate the cost implications of shifting 15–30 percent of their production capacity from China to Southeast Asia (Li and Cheng, 2019). Apple's major contract manufacturer Foxconn has begun assembling the iPhone 11 series at its plant in India, part of supply chain redeployment by the US technology giant to diversify production beyond China (Marandi, 2020). iPhones labeled as being "Design in California Assembled in India" will soon be available on international markets. Foxconn, Apple's most important supplier, has been preparing for the inevitable decoupling of Chinese and American supply chains. As a result, nearly one-third of its production capacity has been outside of China (Li, 2020).

Such relocation is not limited to American companies. Many Japanese companies have sped up their China exit in anticipation of further escalation of the trade war. Nintendo, which had most of its Switch games assembled in China, started moving production to

Vietnam; Sharp considered relocating production of its Dynabook laptop to Vietnam or Taiwan; and Ricoh shifted production of US-bound multifunction printers from China to Thailand (Sese, 2019). According to a research by Nikkei (Hoshi *et al.*, 2020), more than 50 global companies had announced plans to move production out of China. Even Chinese company Goerteck, a major contract manufacturer of wireless earphones for Apple, has relocated its assembly lines to Vietnam to elude the 25 percent tariff, which covers popular AirPods. Table 8.1 lists some of the global companies pulling out of China in face of the trade war. Besides dodging the tariff, maintaining the eligibility for US government procurement is another reason of the China exodus.

Clearly the trade war has been reshaping China-centered value chains. The Kearney China Diversification Index (CDI), which tracks the rebalancing of US manufacturing imports from China to other Asian low cost countries (LCCs), shows that US companies substantially reduced the volume of goods sourced from China, and

Table 8.1   Global companies moving supply chains out of China

Company	Locations	Products
Pegatron (Taiwan)	India	Telecom equipment
Skechers (US)	India	Shoes
Apple	India	Latest iPhone model
Casio (Japan)	Thailand	Wrist watches
Richo (Japan)	Thailand	Printers
Panasonic (Japan)	Thailand	Stereos
Compal Electronics (Taiwan)	Taiwan	Routers
HP (US)	Taiwan	Personal Computers
Dell (US)	Taiwan	Personal Computers
Sharp (Japan)	Vietnam	Personal Computers
Nintendo (Japan)	Vietnam	Video game consoles
GoerTek (China)	Vietnam	iPods
Nidec (Japan)	Mexico	Auto parts
GoPro (US)	Mexico	Small video cameras

Source: Hoshi, Nakafuji and Cho (2020).

began sourcing those goods from other Asian countries. According to the CDI, in 2013 China accounted for 67 percent of manufactured goods exports from Asian LCCs to the US. In 2019, however, China's Q4 share slipped to 56 percent, and the value of US manufactured imports from Asian LCC countries fell from $816 billion in 2018 to $757 billion, a decrease of about 7 percent. This fall was exclusively driven by the sharp contraction of imports from China, which saw Chinese manufactured goods exports to the US tumbled 17 percent, or $90 billion. On the other hand, manufactured goods shipments to the US by other Asian LCCs rose $31 billion in the same year, with Vietnam being the largest beneficiary of the redeployment of the China-centered GVCs: of the $31 billion in US-bound exports diverted from China, Vietnam took over some $14 billion (Kearney, 2020).

The trade war also highlights another risk of GVC strategy: unexpected sanctions on core technology modules, motivated by geopolitical considerations. Firms adopting GVC strategy primarily concentrate on their core competence and source other necessary services and technology modules from suppliers in international markets. GVC strategy depends on two conditions: that transactions between buyers and sellers in international markets are not subject to non-market forces; and that there is no discrimination against buyers on the basis of nationality. Chinese ICT firms such as Lenovo, Huawei, Xiaomi and OPPO have risen in the global market, but that rise is heavily dependent on sourced foreign technologies, most of which are supplied by American MNCs. As the trade war escalated and morphed into a technology leadership war between China and the US, the Trump administration blacklisted more and more Chinese companies, basically prohibiting exports of any American technology to these Chinese companies. As the technology superpower in the world, the US has monopolized core intellectual properties of ICT. Without the operating systems created by American companies, largely Apple, Google and Microsoft, computers and smartphones would be reduced to a collection of electronic components, unable to function as the tools indispensable for work and daily life in the information era. The US sanctions are destructive for Chinese firms who have adopted GVC strategy and have grown highly dependent on American technologies.

In May 2019, the US Department of Commerce (2019) placed Huawei and its affiliates on the Entity List, because it believes that Huawei and its affiliates had been involved in "activities contrary to the national security or foreign policy interests of the United States." The placement on the Entity List has essentially denied Huawei access to American technologies. Even though Huawei is one of the most innovative telecommunications equipment makers in the world, American technologies such as Qualcomm chipsets, Micron memory chips, and Google's Android operating system are indispensable for Huawei products. There is no universally accepted standard of national security. Each sovereign government has the freedom to define national security in accordance with its national interests and priorities. Banning Huawei products from the US market may sound reasonable, equivalent to the Chinese government banning Google, Facebook and Twitter in China.

Huawei is an international company, serving not only American consumers but also consumers in China, Japan, Europe and other non-US markets. The ban on Huawei's access to US technology deprives Huawei of the ability to serve non-US markets, such as the Chinese market. It was estimated that the Trump administration's blacklisting of Huawei could cause a fall of 40–60 million units in annual international shipments of Huawei smartphones (Bloomberg, 2019b). The ban has forced Huawei to shift significantly away from American suppliers, and to accelerate its own development of processor chips and other vital smartphone components. The teardown analysis of the Huawei Mate 30, a 5G-compatible, top of the range smartphone in the Chinese market, shows that American-made parts now constitute only one percent of the total bill of materials, down sharply from the recent figure of 11 percent (Nikkei, 2020).

In May 2020, the US government further constrained Huawei's access to American technology. The US Department of Commerce (2020) issued a new rule requiring that foreign chipmakers who use American design tools or equipment to produce chips for Huawei and its affiliates must apply for licenses. This applies to Huawei's chip design arm, HiSilicon, which has successfully designed its own Kirin series of mobile chips as substitutes for Qualcomm and contracted the manufacture of the chips to Taiwan Semiconductor Manufacturing Company (TSMC), which uses machinery supplied by American company Applied Materials. The new rule basically bars companies around the world from using American-made machinery and software to design or produce chips for Huawei or its affiliates. US software, intellectual property, chip design tools and materials are used by everyone from Qualcomm to Samsung to MediaTek to Sony. The reinforced sanction on Huawei by the Trump administration has inflicted further damage on the largest Chinese telecommunications equipment maker, perhaps even putting its survival in question. As a lead firm, Huawei purchased $26.4 billion worth of parts from Japanese, Taiwanese and Korean companies annually. Sony alone sold billions of dollars worth of smartphone image sensors to Huawei each year; TSMC was estimated to earn over $5 billion in annual sales from Huawei; and Samsung had been a major supplier of memory chips for Huawei (Shimizu, 2020). The new sanction against Huawei has imposed huge collateral damages on all the firms involved in the value chains led by Huawei.

There has always been concern that American companies might suddenly stop providing China with the technologies it needs, thus crippling the Chinese economy. For this reason China crafted its *Made in China 2025* strategy in 2015, which outlines the Chinese industrial policy over the next 10 years, emphasizing the development of future oriented industries: integrated circuits, artificial intelligence, robotics, biotechnology, aerospace equipment, new energy vehicles and new materials. *Made in China 2025* includes the aim of achieving 40 percent Chinese self-sufficiency in core parts and basic materials for those industries by 2020, and 70 percent self-sufficiency by 2025 (China State Council, 2015). The Chinese government regards *Made in China 2025* as insurance that China needs to protect itself against plausible hostile technology blockades. In the past, many Chinese scholars and government officials voiced the opinion that such risk was slim, seeing that kind of concern as a remnant of cold war mentality. The attack on

Huawei, after a similar attack on ZTE in 2018, suggests that the risk is real. The Huawei and ZTE incidents should definitely alert the Chinese government to the risk of excessive dependence on US technology, and should motivate China to pursue self-sufficiency and independence in core technologies — which will in turn weaken and challenge the technology monopoly enjoyed by American companies. As more and more Chinese high-technology companies have been included in the Entity list administrated by the US Commerce Department, the decoupling of Chinese and US technology sectors will have been inevitable, which will surely encourage China to pursue an inward-looking technology development policy, and may discourage Chinese firms, especially high-technology ones, from following GVC-based growth strategy. The forced US–China decoupling by the Trump administration may end up hurting the US more than China. According to Boston Consulting Group, over the next three to five years, US chipmakers would suffer a 16 percent drop in revenue if the US were to maintain its current restrictions, and a 37 percent drop in revenue if the US completely banned chipmakers from selling to Chinese customers (Tan, 2020).

The COVID-19 pandemic: A second shock for China-centered GVCs

On January 15, 2020, the US and China signed a phase one trade deal, agreeing to a temporary truce in the trade war. It was expected that the truce might mitigate the uncertainty of economic relations between the two nations. Unfortunately, the COVID-19 pandemic, which originated in Wuhan, China, heralded a new risk for Chinese-centered GVCs. By October 2020 the coronavirus had infected more than 50 million people worldwide, with deaths numbering more than one million. The worldwide spread of the virus has caused serious disruption to economic activities of the global economy. The economic contagion of the coronavirus has been spreading quickly along GCVs. The lockdown of Wuhan and restrictions on personal mobility within China virtually froze the

Chinese economy, leading to the shutdown of upstream foreign factories in various nations who relied on Chinese-made parts and components.

Assembly of ready-to-use products is one dimension of the importance of China-centered GVCs. Chinese firms' involvement in GVCs has expanded beyond mere assembly. Supplying parts and components to foreign firms in the upper reaches of value chains is now another dimension of China's activity. Continuous technology innovation has enhanced the production capacities of Chinese firms to include intermediate inputs, and the reliance of the world economy on intermediate materials from China had risen dramatically in the last two decades. In 2017, China produced 9.6 percent of the world's intermediate imports, much higher than the 4 percent of 2003, the year when the SARS virus emerged and spread. Compared with the world average, the dependence of East and Southeast Asian countries on China is even higher, given the regional bias of value chains. For Southeast Asian countries, China has replaced Japan as the most important external supplier of intermediate materials.

Figure 8.1 shows the importance of China as a supplier of intermediate goods to the world economy. One-fifth of Japanese intermediate imports came from China in 2017, and the same was true

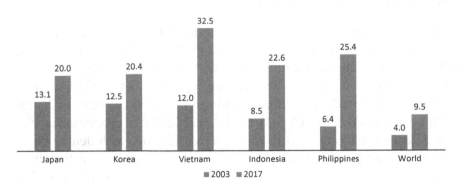

Figure 8.1   Imports of intermediate goods from China by country (Percentage of total intermediate imports)

Source: The author's calculations with World Bank data.

for Korean intermediate imports. Southeast Asian countries saw a sharp rise in intermediate imports from China during the period 2003–2017. The share of Chinese goods in Indonesian intermediate imports rose from 8.5 to 22.6 percent, while that of the Philippines jumped from 6.4 to 25.4 percent. The reliance of Vietnam on Chinese intermediates was the highest among all East and Southeast Asian countries: in 2017, almost one-third of Vietnam's intermediate imports came from China. In value chains involving both Chinese and Vietnamese firms, such as electronics and apparel value chains, the Chinese firms are positioned in relatively high value-added segments, providing intermediate inputs to upstream firms located in Vietnam. Vietnam has emerged as the second largest mobile phone exporter in the world, since Samsung has relocated all of its Chinese assembly factories to Vietnam. However, parts and components such as batteries and memory chips manufactured in Samsung's Chinese factories are indispensable for assembly in the plants in Vietnam.

Moreover, recently China has been the world's largest exporter of motor vehicle parts and accessories, with an export volume of $34.8 billion in 2018. Figure 8.2 displays American, Japanese, German, and Korean imports of motor vehicle parts and accessories from China. The American auto industry was the most reliant on

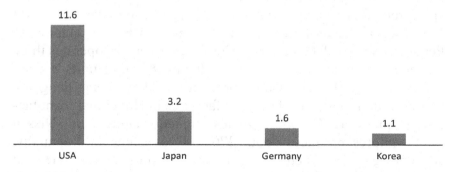

Figure 8.2 Motor vehicle parts and accessories imported from China in 2018 by country (Billion US dollar)

Source: UNCOMTRADE database.

China, with $11.6 billion in motor vehicle parts and accessories imported from China, accounting for 16.2 percent of total US imports in that category. Japan imported $3.2 billion in vehicle parts and accessories from China, much less than the US. However, in terms of percentage of total imports, China contributed more than one-third of Japanese imports of motor vehicle parts and accessories. Japanese exposure to the risk of production disruption in the Chinese auto industry is the largest of all major automobile producing countries.

The automobile industry is a pillar industry and growth engine of the Korean economy. For some time now, Chinese parts suppliers have been deeply involved in the value chains of Korean automobile companies. In 2018, Korea imported $1.1 billion worth of motor vehicle parts and accessories from China, about 28.1 percent of Korean imports in that category. It was reported that Chinese factories supply 87 percent of the wire harness used by Korean car makers. German automakers, on the other hand, are the least reliant on Chinese suppliers; in 2018, China exported $1.6 billion in motor vehicle parts and accessories to Germany, only about 3.6 percent of total German imports of such goods.

Hubei Province, the Chinese province hardest hit by the pandemic, is an important hub of the Chinese automobile industry. It produced 2.25 million vehicles in 2019, about 9 percent of China's total output for that year. Dong Feng Motor, one of China's top state-owned automakers, is located in Hubei's Wuhan City, the epicenter of the coronavirus. Dong Feng has joint ventures with Japanese car makers Honda and Nissan, and French automaker Peugeot-Citroen. A Dong Feng–Honda joint venture operates three passenger car plants in Hubei, producing 800,000 units a year, nearly half of Honda's China production. Dong Feng–Peugeot–Citroen Automobile also has three factories in Hubei that manufacture as many as 750,000 vehicles annually. Dong Feng–Nissan joint ventures produces about 270,000 passenger cars annually, accounting for 20 percent of Nissan's China output. General Motors produces Chevrolet and Buick branded cars in Hubei through its joint venture with SAIC Motor (Boston Consulting Group, 2020).

The lockdown in Hubei Province, the epicenter of the pandemic, immediately triggered disruptions in the operations of the automobile industry worldwide. Nissan Motor suspended production at a plant in Kyushu, Japan, because of the likelihood of difficulty in procuring parts from China as a result of supply chain disruption; Toyota Motor stopped some production at facilities including its Shimoyama factory, it also shut down its four Chinese auto-manufacturing plants. South Korea's Hyundai Motor suspended operations at its three domestic auto assembly plants (Okada, 2020; Koizumi *et al.*, 2020).

The spread of the coronavirus in China caused closures of Chinese factories nation-wide, which prompted domino effects in the rest of the world. From 11 to 14 February, 2020, the American Chamber of Commerce in Shanghai (2020) surveyed 109 American companies in Shanghai and neighboring provinces to get an understanding of the operation environment under the impact of the COVID-19 pandemic. Among the firms surveyed, 48 percent reported that their global operations had been affected by the lockdown in response to the spread of the coronavirus. Among this 48 percent, 78 percent indicated that they did not have sufficient workers to resume full production line operations. Shanghai Japanese Commerce and Industry Club conducted a similar survey regarding the operations of Japanese companies in China. The results imply that the COVID-19 outbreak had affected the supply chains of 54 percent of surveyed companies, and that only 23 percent had alternative procurement plans in the case of prolonged factory shutdowns in China (Nakafuji and Moriyasu, 2020).

China is Apple's biggest production hub: 75 percent of Apple's top 200 suppliers had at least one factory in China. Chinese factory shutdowns and slow resumption of operations due to the outbreak disrupted Apple supply chains. Apple (2020) warned investors that the revenue target for March 2020, announced in January, would not be achieved. To meet the rising demand for AirPods, the most popular wireless earphones for smartphones, Apple planned to drastically increase AirPod production, with a target of 45 million units in the first half of 2020. However, the COVID-19 pandemic forced

Luxshare Precision Industry, Goertek and Inventec, the three key manufacturers of AirPods in China, to shut down for two more weeks after the end of the Lunar New Year holiday in 2020.

Fast Retailing, the owner of the casual wear brand UNIQLO, had 128 factories in China, accounting for more than half of its contract manufacturers. It announced on the company's website that "There are delays in production and logistics due to the coronavirus." About 20 percent of UNIQLO's sewing factories were in Vietnam; those factories were highly dependent on raw materials from China. The virus-induced lockdown in China disrupted the supply of Chinese made fabrics and caused shipments from Vietnamese sewing factories to be delayed. Contract manufacturers for American brands such as GAP and Tommy Hilfiger were also facing a shortage of Chinese fabrics. According to Cambodia Garment Manufacturers Association, Cambodia's apparel industry garment makers purchase some 60 percent of their raw materials from China. The economic contagion of the COVID-19 impacted the normal business activities of the Cambodian garment industry. About 200 factories with 90,000 workers would be suspended if new Chinese supplies did not arrive (Onish and Okutsu, 2020).

The ongoing China–US trade war has triggered the redeployment of value chains away from China. The pandemic has further exacerbated the exodus of foreign companies from China. In a February 2020 survey by the American Chamber of Commerce in Shanghai (2020), 30 percent of the firms surveyed stated that they planned to shift their production out of China if their factories were unable to re-open. Google and Microsoft are two significant newcomers to the manufacture of smartphones and personal computers. In light of emerging COVID-19 ramifications, Google and Microsoft accelerated their efforts to shift production of their new phones, personal computers and other devices from China to Southeast Asia. Google shipped seven million mobile phones in 2019; Microsoft six million personal computers in the same year. Most of those Google smartphones and Microsoft-built computers were made in China. Those two newcomers to the hardware sector had planned to shift production out of China because of the US–China trade war. The COVID-19 outbreak strengthened their determination to diversify their production bases away from China. It was reported that after the closure of Chinese factories due to the outbreak of the COVID-19, Google even requested its Chinese suppliers to evaluate the feasibility and cost implications of shipping production equipment from China to Vietnam (Chen and Li, 2020).

Japanese manufacturers started to shift production out of China, as worries mounted that the deadly virus outbreak could prolong plant closures in China. According to the chief financial officer of Panasonic, the company had prepared an alternative production plan outside China for electronic products. Aisin Seiki Co., a major Japanese auto parts maker, moved some of its Chinese lines back to Japan so as to cope with the COVID-19 disruption. Toyota Boshoku Corp., which had extensive operations in China, considered shifting production back to Japan or to Thailand. Some Japanese companies, such as Nintendo, Sharp and Ricoh, had started to move their production out of China after the eruption of China–US trade war. All these Japanese companies have accelerated their exodus (Horiuchi, 2020). The COVID-19 pandemic is another demonstration that excessive dependence on China is risky, and that diversification is an essential element of strategy for coping with political and natural disasters.

The COVID-19 pandemic exposes the danger of medical supply chains

The COVID-19 pandemic reveals the danger of excessive reliance on China for the supply of essential medical goods. All countries hit by the pandemic saw a sudden surge in demand for ventilators and personal protective equipment — they had insufficient domestic capacity to produce those goods, and had to depend heavily on imports, mostly from China. The pandemic threatened smooth and sustainable supply of those goods. The structural principle of GVCs is to disperse all manufacturing tasks globally, in line with the comparative advantage of individual countries, and ship products to international markets in accordance with pre-concluded agreements. Hand sanitizers, personal protective equipment and ventilators have long been considered standard commodities; in recent decades, most developed countries had offshored or outsourced the production of those goods to developing countries, with China a main contract producer.

Two turns of events resulting from the unexpected outbreak of the COVID-19 highlighted the risks inherent in excessive alliance on China for the supply of medical goods. First, the outbreak of the COVID-19 triggered a spike in demand for personal protective equipment, ventilators and other essential medical goods, which immediately caused shortages. The import-dependent countries were shocked to find that they could not increase their domestic production of those goods because they lacked the basic production facilities. They had to import that infrastructure from abroad, mostly from China.

Second, because the major supplier, China, was hit first by the COVID-19, the expected smooth and sustainable supply flows were in jeopardy. The lockdown in Wuhan and the strict nation-wide isolation policy seriously disrupted production in Chinese factories. Even worse, when China was fighting the COVID-19 spread, Chinese demand for personal protective equipment and ventilators increased astronomically. The Chinese government prioritized domestic demand for these products over foreign demand. Made in China goods evolved to "used in China," which further intensified the shortage of those goods globally. For instance, Canadian mask maker Medicom Group was forced to sell outputs from its Shanghai factory to the local Shanghai government (Imahashi and Phoonphongphipha, 2020), revealing an unexpected risk inherent in reliance on China as a global supplier.

As a matter of fact, it was not just the Chinese government that interfered in the operations of the value chains manufacturing medical supplies during the pandemic. The Taiwanese government, worried about the shortage of masks, in January 2020 banned the export of masks. ST Technology, a Singapore government affiliated company, had two mask production lines in Taiwan. The Singapore government asked the company to ramp up mask production after the outbreak of the COVID-19 in Wuhan, China. The masks were scheduled to be shipped to Singapore after the Chinese Lunar New Year in 2020, but the ban by the Taiwanese government made it impossible to ship the masks to Singapore with the planned timing. As a workaround, ST Technology shifted its production lines back to Singapore (Sim, 2020). The same thing happened in the US: President Trump attempted to use the Defense Production Act to block American company 3M from shipping N95 masks to Canada and Europe, neither of which had domestic facilities for the production of masks.

Moreover, China has been an important source of APIs, materials necessary for the manufacture of drugs. In Hubei, the epidemic center, were there 44 pharmaceutical manufacturing facilities approved by the US Food and Drug Administration or by its European counterpart to make products for the US and European markets. Of those, 35 were API producers. Closure of those factories disrupted pharmaceutical supply chains and threatened to cause shortages of drugs dependent on Chinese-made API. In the US, 80 percent of antibiotics came from China, including 95 percent of ibuprofen, 91 percent of hydrocortisone and 45 percent of penicillin (McGinley and Johnson, 2020). India, the world's largest generic drug maker, purchases 70 percent of the APIs used by its own pharmaceutical industry from China. Worried about the disruption of the API supply, the Indian government restricted the export of medicines made with Chinese-made APIs (Ellis-Petersen, 2020). It is natural that sovereign governments put the welfare of their own people first, as in the America First movement promoted by President Trump, directing domestically produced goods to serve domestic demand first when pandemic-related shortages arise. However, such government intervention endangers those countries which have no domestic production facilities and depend on foreign imports.

Responses to the pandemic-related shortages of key medical items vary from country to country. In the wake of the pandemic, France's Finance Minister Bruno Lemaire, formerly an enthusiastic advocate of free and unbridled competition, called for a rethink of globalization and criticized Europe's over-reliance on China as "irresponsible and unreasonable." Christoph Stoller, the President of Medicines for Europe, which represents the generics industry, urged the repatriation of the production of essential APIs to Europe (Lorin, 2020).

Under the code name Project Defend, British Prime Minister Boris Johnson instructed his administration to investigate the reliance of the UK on Chinese supplies of medical goods, pharmaceutical products and other strategic imports, and to draft a strategy to end excessive dependence on China. Project Defend is part of a new broad approach to national security directed by UK Foreign Secretary Dominic Raab (*Reuters*, 2020).

US trade representative Robert Lighthizer stated that "overdependence on other countries as a source of cheap medical products and supplies has created a strategic vulnerability" in the US economy. President Trump's advisor Peter Navarro, who has been calling to the reshoring of supply chains, described the pandemic as a wake-up call for the US to reduce its reliance on pharmaceutical and medical imports from China (Williams, 2020). On August 6, 2020, President Trump signed an executive order requiring US Federal government agencies, to buy essential medicines, medical equipment and protective gear made in the US. The executive order intends to bring pharmaceutical and medical supply chains home, reassert American economic independence and end reliance on China (Levy and Hopkins, 2020).

The Japanese government launched a stimulus package of 2 trillion yen to cope with the economic contagion of the pandemic; to date, it has allocated 245.6 billion Japanese yen to help Japanese companies to move their Chinese production facilities back home or relocate them to ASEAN countries. Specifically, the Japanese government has promised to pay half to two-thirds of relocation costs for companies moving their production of masks, sanitizers, ventilators, ECOM and other medical equipment essential to human health back to Japan. Also, if Japanese companies expand their API production capacity, which is highly dependent on imports, the Japanese government will subsidize 50 percent of the required investment. In the first round of applications closed in June 2020, the Japanese government approved 57 projects totaling 57.4 billion yen for shifting production facilities back to Japan. In the second round of applications ended in July, there were 1,670 applications worth about 1.76 trillion yen — 11 times of the remaining amount in the budget (Akiyama, 2020). In an expansion of the subsidy program aiming at diversifying supply chains, the Japanese government has included India and Bangladesh as eligible destinations for Japanese companies leaving China. Following the decision of the Japanese government, Indian Prime Minister Narendra Modi proposed reshaping global supply chains based on trust and stability, not just costs and benefits when he addressed to the US–India Strategic Partnership Forum (Sharma and Gakuto, 2020).

Without doubt, production costs will rise if supply chains of medical goods and pharmaceutical products are relocated from China to Japan, the UK and the US. The loss of economic efficiency in the manufacture of those goods will be a built-in cost of reshoring. However, sovereign governments always prioritize national security over economic efficiency. Food and energy are conventional strategic commodities considered vital to national security. Almost all countries strive to maintain food self-sufficiency and build up oil reserves as precautionary measures, without consideration of economic efficiency. Medical equipment and drugs had never been on the list of commodities designated as essential to national security. The shortages of basic medical supplies during the pandemic have taught all governments a lesson: depending on GVCs for essential medical supplies is not wise; in fact it is dangerous. In the future, more and more sovereign governments may treat medical goods and essential drugs as equal in importance to food and energy, adding them to the list of products essential for national security. Reshoring the production of personal protective equipment, ventilators, APIs and other primary medical goods is expected to be part of a new trend, and GVC restructuring to reduce developed countries' reliance on China for medical goods will inevitably undermine the central status of China in GVCs.

Conclusion

GVC strategy has facilitated China's industrialization and nurtured the Chinese export miracle in the last four decades. However, it is not without risk. Natural disasters and geopolitical tensions can easily disrupt the smooth operations and reliable production of GVCs. Recently, China-centered GCVs have been facing two major sources of risk: the US–China trade war and the COVID-19 pandemic. Maximization of the economic benefits of global production fragmentation had driven the worldwide proliferation of GVCs, but MNCs failed to give sufficient consideration to the accompanying risks that could suddenly undermine the reliability of GVCs. To date, for many governments and MNCs, the costs of those risks have greatly outweighed the economic benefits of partaking in China-centered GVCs. Now, a geographic restructuring of the allocation of value chains is imperative for a balancing of risks and benefits. This will determine the future trajectory of GVCs.

The 25 percent tariff imposed by the Trump administration on $250 billion in Chinese goods has prompted some MNCs to shift their production capacities out of China or reduce the volume of goods they contract to be produced there. The pandemic experience has shown that diversification of supply chains is critical for coping with unexpected natural disasters. Excessive reliance on one country, such as China, is very risky. The disruption of one segment of a value chain, regardless of its technological importance, can cause the shutdown of all firms involved in that chain. Medical goods such as sanitizers, personal protective equipment, ventilators and APIs, all essential for the protection of human health, would be put on each nation's list of goods essential for national security, and treated as important as food and energy. Reduction of reliance on GVCs by reshoring production will highly likely be a new trend. These two believable predictions suggest that the importance of China as a dominant supplier in GVCs is likely to gradually diminish.

For Chinese high-technology companies on the Entity list such as Huawei, the US sanctions on imports of American technologies mean the end of GVC strategy. Those high-technology Chinese companies will have to invest massively in R&D and pursue self-independence in key areas crucial to future development, including core ICT, artificial intelligence and bio-technology. The decoupling of China and the US in value chains of technology products will be inevitable. The era in which Chinese firms could easily leverage American technology to achieve their own industrialization and catch-up has ended.

Bibliography

Adams, G. F., Ganges, B. and Shachmurove, Y. (2006), "Why is China so competitive? Measuring and explaining China's competitiveness," *World Economy*, 29(2): 95–122.

Adler, G., Meleshchuk, S. and Buitron, C. O. (2019), "Global value chains and external adjustment: Do exchange rates still matter?" *IMF Working Paper*, WP/19/300.

Ahmed, S., Appendino, M. and Ruta, M. (2015), "Global value chains and the exchange rate elasticity of exports," *IMF Working Paper*, WP/15/252.

Akiyama, H. (2020), "Japan companies line up for 'China exit' subsidies to come home," *Nikkei Asian Review*, September 9, 2020.

American Chamber of Commerce in China (2019), *Joint Press Release*, May 22, 2019.

American Chamber of Commerce in Shanghai (2020), "Supply chains and factory openings: An AmCham Shanghai mini-survey," https://www.amcham-shanghai.org/en/preview (accessed on February 28, 2020).

Apple (2020), "Press release: Investor update on quarterly guidance," February 17, 2020.

Baldwin, R. (2016), *The Great Convergence: Information Technology and the New Globalization*, Harvard University Press, Harvard.

Baldwin, R. (2018), "A long view of globalization in short: The new globalization, Part 5 of 5," *VOXEU*, December 5, 2018.

Baldwin, C. Y. and Clark, K. B. (1997), "Managing in an age of modularity," *Harvard Business Review*, September–October, 1997.

Backer, K. D. (2011), "Global value chains: Preliminary evidence and policy issues," http://www.oecd.org/industry/ind/47945400.pdf (accessed on February 14, 2020).

Basker, E. and Pham, V. H. (2007), "Wal-Mart as catalyst to US–China trade," https://ssrn.com/abstract=987583.

Bayard, K., Byrne, D. and Smith, D. (2015), "The Scope of U.S. factoryless maufacturing," in S. N. Houseman and M. Mandel (eds.), *Measuring Globalization: Better Trade Statistics for Better Policy*, Vol. 2, Upjohn Institute for Employment Research.

Beeny, T., Bisceglie, J., Wildasin, B. and Cheng, D. (2018), "Supply chain vulnerabilities from China in U.S. Federal information and communication technology," US–China Economic and Security Review Commission, US House of Representatives.

Bems, R. and Johnson, R. (2012), "Value-added exchange rates," VoxEU.org, December 6, 2012.

Berger, B. and Martin, R. F. (2013), "The Chinese export boom: An examination of the detailed trade data," *China and the World Economy*, 21(1): 64–90.

Bernanke, S. B. (2005), "The global saving glut and the US current account deficit," Remarks at the Sandridge Lecture, Virginia Association of Economists, Richmond, Virginia.

Bernanke, S. B. (2009), "Financial reform to address systemic risk," Speech at the Council on Foreign Relations, Washington DC, March 10.

Bernard, A. B., Jensen, J. B., Redding, S. J. and Schoott, P. K. (2010), "Wholesalers and retailers in US trade," *American Economic Review*, 100(2): 408–413.

Bloomberg (2019a), "No pay, no gain: Huawei outspends Apple on R&D for a 5G edge," https://www.bloomberg.com/news/articles/2019-04-25/huawei-s-r-d-spending-balloons-as-u-s-tensions-flare-over-5g (accessed on July 18, 2019).

Bloomberg (2019b), "Huawei braces for phone sales drop of up to 60 million overseas," June 17, 2019, https://www.bloomberg.com/news/articles/2019-06-16/huawei-braces-for-a-steep-drop-in-overseas-smartphone-sales.

Bongiorni, S. (2008), *A Year Without Made in China: One Family's True Life Adventure in the Global Economy*, Wiley, Hoboken.

Bordo, M. D. and McCauley, R. N. (2017), "Triffin: Dilemma or myth?" *BIS Working Paper No. 684*, December 19, 2017, https://www.bis.org/publ/work684.htm.

Boston Consulting Group (2020), "The Impact of COVID-19 on the Chinese automotive industry," June 1, 2020.

Branstetter, L. and Lardy, N. (2006), "China's embrace of globalization," *NBER Working Paper* 12373.

Brambilla, I., Khandelwal, A. K. and Schoot, P. K. (2009), "China's experience under the Multiber Arrangement (MFA) and the Agreement on Textiles and Clothing (ATC)," in Robert Feenstra and Shang-Jin Wei (eds.), *China's Growing Role in World Trade*, University of Chicago Press, Chicago.

Brandt, L. and Thun, E. (2011), "Going mobile in China: Shifting value chains and upgrading in the mobile telecom sector," *International Journal of Technological Learning, Innovation and Development*, 4: 148–180.

Bronnenberg, B. J., Dube, J. H. and Gentzkow, M. (2012), "The evolution of brand preference: Evidence from consumer migration," *American Economic Review*, 102(6): 2472–2508.

Candytech (2020), "Smartphone market share India — 2020 (Samsung loses, Xiomi and Realme gains)," https://candytech.in/smartphone-market-share-india/.

China Daily (2019), "Ten policies and measures on foreign investment," November 11, 2019, https://www.chinadaily.com.cn/regional/2019-11/28/content_37526187.htm.

China State Council (2015), "Made in China 2025," http://www.gov.cn/zhengce/content/2015-05/19/content_9784.htm.

Chen, S. and Wen, P. (2013), "The development and evolution of China's mobile phone industry," *Working Paper Series No. 2013-1*, Chung-Hua Institute for Economics Research.

Chen, T. and Li, L. (2020), "Google, Microsoft shift production from China faster due to virus," *Nikkei Asian Review*, February 26, 2020.

Cheung, Y., Qian, X. and Chinn, M. D. (2015), "China–US trade flow behaviors: The implications of alternative exchange rate measures and trade classifications," *Review of World Economics*, 152(1): 43–67.

Cline, W. R. (2010), "Renminbi undervaluation, China's surplus, and the US trade deficit," *Policy Brief No. PB10-20*, Peterson Institute for International Economics.

Chipman, I. (2019), "The power of brands, conscious and unconscious," *Knowable Magazine*, 2 February, 2019.

Chow, G. C. (1994), *Understanding China's Economy*, World Scientific, Singapore.

Counterpoint (2019), "Global smartphone market share by quarter," https://www.counterpointresearch.com/global-smartphone-share/ (accessed on July 11, 2019).

Counterpoint (2020a), "China smartphone market share: by quarter," https://www.counterpointresearch.com/china-smartphone-share/.

Counterpoint (2020b), "Global smartphone market share: By quarter," https://www.counterpointresearch.com/global-smartphone-share/#:~:text=Q4%20 2019%20Highlights&text=Global%20smartphone%20shipments%20 reached%20401,other%20brands%20to%20compete%20fiercely.

Credit Suisse (2010), *The Power of Brand Investing*, Credit Suisse Research Institute, Zurich.

Dai, M., Maitra, M. and Yu, M. (2016), "Unexceptional exporter performance in China? The role of processing trade," *Journal of Development Economics*, 123: 177–189.

The Economist (2009), "When a flow becomes a flood," *Economists*, January, 22, 2009.

Edmonds, C. M., Croix, S. J. and Li, Y. (2006), *China's Rise as an International Trading Power*, East-West Center, Hononluu.

Ellis-Petersen, H. (2020), "India limits medicine exports after supplies hit by coronavirus," https://www.theguardian.com/world/2020/mar/04/india-limits-medicine-exports-coronavirus-paracetamol-antibiotics.

Dedrick, J., Kraemer, K. L. and Linden, G. (2010), "Who profits from innovation in global value chains? A study of the iPod and notebook PCs," *Industrials and Corporate Change*, 19(1): 81–116.

ESCAP (2015), *Asia-Pacific Trade and Investment Report 2015*.

Egan, M. L. and Mody, A. (1992), " Buyer-seller links in export development," *World Development*, 20(3): 321–334.

Engel, C. (2006), "Equivalent results for optimal pass-through, optimal indexing to exchange rates, and optimal choice of currency for export pricing," *Journal of European Economic Association*, 4(6): 1249–1260.

Ferguson, N. and Schularick, M. (2009), "The end of Chimerica," *Harvard Business School BGIE Unit Working Paper No. 10-037*.

Finder (2019), "iPhone sales statistics: Just how popular is Apple's smartphone in the US?" https://www.finder.com/iphone-sales-statistics (accessed on September 20, 2019).

Frankel, J. (2009), "Eight reasons we are given not to worry about the US deficits," *Working Paper No. 58*, The Commission on Growth and Development.

Gereffi, G. (1999), "International trade and industrial upgrading in the apparel commodity chain," *Journal of International Economics*, 48: 37–70.

Gereffi, G. and Christian, M. M. (2009), "The impacts of Wal-Mart: The rise and consequences of the world's dominant retailer," *Annual Review of Sociology*, 35, August.

Gereffi, G. and Karina, F. (2011), *Global Value Chain Analysis: A Primer, Center on Globalization, Governance and Competitiveness*, Duke University, Durham.

Gereffi, G., Humphrey, J and Sturgeon, T (2005), "The governance of global value chain," *Review of International Political Economy*, 12(1): 78–104.

Godin, B. (2006), "The linear model of innovation: The historical construction of an analytical framework," *Science, Technology, and Human Values*, 31(6): 639–667.

Grimes, S. and Sun, Y. (2016), "China's evolving role in Apple's global value chain," *Area Development and Policy*, 1(1), 94–112.

Goldberg, L. S. and Tille, C. (2005), Vehicle currency use in international trade. *NBER Working Paper No. 11127*. Cambridge, NBER.

Goldberg, P. K. and Knetter, M. M. (1997), "Good prices and exchange rates: What have we learned," *Journal of Economic Literature*, XXXV: 1243–1272.

Goldstein, M. and Lardy, N. (2009), "China's exchange rate policy dilemma," *American Economic Review*, 96(2): 422–426.

Grossman G. M. and Rossi-Hansberg, E. (2008), "Trading tasks: A simple theory of offshoring," *American Economic Review*, 98(5): 1978–1997.

Horiuchi, J. (2020), "Japan firms weigh production shift out of China as virus wreaks havoc," *Kyodo News*, February 7, 2020.

Hoshi, M., Nakafuji, R. and Cho, Y. (2020), "China scrambles to stem manufacturing exodus as 50 companies leave," *Nikkei Asian Review*, July 18, 2019.

Hu, Z. F. and Khan, M. (1997), "Why is China growing so fast?" *IMF Staff Papers*, 44(1): 103–131.

Hu, J., Wan, H. and Zhu, H. (2011), "The business model of a Shanzai mobile phone firm in China," *Australian Journal of Business and Management Research*, 1(3): 53–61.

IDC (2019), "Lenovo reclaims the #1 spot in PC ranking in Q3 2019," https://www.idc.com/getdoc.jsp?containerId=prUS44385418 (accessed on July 11, 2019).

Imahashi, R. and Phoonphongphipha, A. (2020), "Mask makers contend with new risk in Asia: State intervention," *Nikkei Asian Review*, March 3, 2020.

Inomata, S. (2017), "Analytical frameworks for global value chains: An overview," in *Global Value Chain Development Report 2017: Measuring and Analyzing the Impact of GVCs on Economic Development*, World Bank.

Isaacson, W. (2011), *Steve Jobs*, Simon & Schuster, New York.

Johnson, R. C. and Noguera, G. (2012), "Accounting for intermediates: Production sharing and trade in value added," *Journal of International Economics*, 86: 224–236.

Kaplinsky, R. (2000), "Globalization and unequalization: What can be learned from value chain analysis?" *The Journal of Development Studies*, 37(2): 117–142.

Kaplinsky, R. (2013), "Global value chains, where they came from where they are going and why this is important," *Working Paper No. 68*, November 2013, Development Policy and Practice, The Open University.

Kapadia, S. (2020), "From Section 301 to COVID-19: How a volatile China changed supply chains," Supply Chain Drive, https://www.supplychaindive.com/news/coronavirus-china-tariff-trade-supply-chains/574702/.

Kearney (2020), "Trade war spurs sharp reversal in 2019 reshoring index, foreshadowing Covid-19 test of supply chain resilience." https://www.kearney.com/operations-performance-transformation/us-reshoring-index/full-report?utm_medium=pr&utm_source=prnewswire&utm_campaign=2020ReshoringIndex.

Koizumi, H., Hosokawa, K. and Tabeta, S. (2020), Automakers count down to looming China parts shortage, *Nikkei Asian Review*, February 5, 2020.

Kowalski, P., Gonzalez, J. L., Ragoussis, A. and Ugarte, C. (2015), "Participation of developing countries in global value chains: Implication for trade and trade related policies," *OECD Trade Policy Papers, No. 179.*

Krugman, P. (2010), "Taking on China," *New York Times*, March 14, 2010. https://www.nytimes.com/2010/03/15/opinion/15krugman.html? src=me.

Lardy, N. R. (2000), "Permanent normal trade relations for China," https://www. brookings.edu/research/permanent-normal-trade-relations-for-china/ *Policy Brief*, 58, May 2000, Brooking Institute.

Lardy, N. R. (2003), *Trade Liberalization and Its Role in Chinese Economic Growth*, Institute for International Economics, Washington DC.

Levy, R. and Hopkins, J. (2020), "Trump signs executive order to boost US production of essential medicine," *Wall Street Journal*, August 6, 2020.

Li, L. (2020), "Foxconn planning for 'inevitable' split between US–China markets," *Nikkei Asian Review*, August 12, 2020.

Li, K. and Cheng, T. (2019), "Apple weights 15%–30% capacity shift out of China," *Nikkei Asian Review*, July 19, 2019.

Li, Y. (2019), "Be vigilant on the evolution of the trade war into a financial war," June 10, 2019, http://www.acfic.org.cn/fgdt1/zjgd/201906/t20190610_128556.html.

Lin, J. Y., Cai, F. and Li, Z. (2003), *The China Miracle*, The Chinese University Press, Hong Kong.

Lorin, V. (2020), "The 'irresponsible' reliance of European big pharma on China," *European Data Journalism Network*, March 11, 2020.

Lu, D. (2010), "Exceptional exporter performance? Evidence from Chinese manufacturing firms," *Working Paper*. https://www.scribd.com/document/48194625/DanLuJMP.

Luo, X. and Xu, X. (2018), "Infrastructure, value chains and economic upgrades," *Journal of Infrastructure, Policy and Development*, 2(2): 1–32.

Ma, H., Wang, Z. and Zhu, K. (2015), "Domestic content in China's exports and its distribution by firm ownership," *Journal of Comparative Economics*, 43(1): 3–18.

McKinnon, R. (2010), "A reply to Kurgman," *International Economy: The Magazine of International Economic Policy*, Winter, 37–39.

Marchi, V. D., Giuliani, E. and Rabellotti, R. (2017), "Global value chains offer developing countries learning and innovation opportunities," *European Journal of Development Research*, December 17.

Malikov, E., Zhao, S. and Kumbhakar, S. C. (2017), "Estimation of firm-level productivity in the presence of exports: Evidence from Chinas manufacturing," *Working Paper*.

Maddison, A. (2001), *The World Economy: A Millennial Perspective*, OECD, Paris.

Marandi, R. (2020), "Made in India iPhone 11 goes into production in Chennai," *Nikkei Asian Weekly*, July 28, 2020.

Marquez, J. and Schindler, J. (2007), "Exchange rate effects on China's trade," *Review of International Economics*, 15(5): 837–853.

McGinley, L. and Johnson, C. Y. (2020), "Coronavirus raises fears of US drug supply disruptions: Many pharmaceuticals' active ingredients are made in China," *Washington Post*, February 27, 2020.

Meri, T. (2009), "China passes the EU in high-tech exports," *Science and Technology, Eurostat Statistics in Focus*.

Merie, R. (2018), "A guide to the financial crisis," *Washington Post*, September 10, 2018, https://www.washingtonpost.com/business/economy/a-guide-to-the-financial-crisis--10-years-later/2018/09/10/114b76ba-af10-11e8-a20b-5f4f84429666_story.html.

Melitz, M. J. (2003), "The impact of trade on intra-industry reallocations and aggregate industry productivity," *Econometrica*, 71(6): 1695–1725.

Morrison, A., Pietrobelli, C. and Rabellotti, R. (2008), "Global value chains and technological capabilities: A framework to study learning and innovation in developing countries," *Oxford Development Studies*, 36(1): 39–58.

Morrison, W. M. (2018), "China–US trade issues," Congressional Research Service report, July 30, 2018.

Murayama, K. and Regalado, F. (2019), "Apple CEO looks at 'all countries' to pick best suppliers," *Nikkei Asian Review*, December 11, 2019.

Nakafuji, R. and Moriyasu, K. (2020), "Multinationals reroute supply chains from China — for good?" *Nikkei Asian Review*, February 15, 2020.

Naughton, B. (1996), "China in the world economy," *Brookings Papers on Economic Activities*: 2273–344.

Nikkei (2020), "Japan reveals 87 projects eligible for 'China exit' subsidies," *Nikkei Asian Review*, July 17, 2020.

Nordas, H. K. (2008), "Gatekeepers to consumer markets: The role of retailers in international trade," *The International Review of Retail Distribution and Research*, 18(5): 449–472.

Obstfeld, M. and Rogoff, K. (2009), "Global imbalances and the financial crisis: Products of common causes," Paper Prepared for the Federal Reserve Bank of San Francisco Asia Economic Policy Conference, Santa Barbara, CA, October 18–20, 2009.

OECD (2015), *Participation of Developing Countries in Global Value Chains: Trade and Trade Relate Policies*, OECD, Paris.

OECD and WTO (2012), "Trade in value-added: Concepts, methodologies and challenges," https://www.oecd.org/sti/ind/49894138.pdf (accessed on February 14, 2020).

Okada, E. (2020), "Mazada delays restart of Chinese factories, amid of coronavirus threat," *Nikkei Asian Review*, February 12, 2020.

Onish, T. and Okutsu, A. (2020), "Southeast Asia's garment supply chain torn up by virus," *Nikkei Asian Review*, February 21, 2020.

Pierce, J. R. and Schott, P. K. (2016), "The surprisingly swift decline of US manufacturing employment," *American Economic Review*, 106(7), 163–162.

Portes, R. (2009), "Global imbalances," in M. Dewatripont, X. Freixas, and R. Portes, (eds.), *Macroeconomic Stability and Financial Regulation: Key Issues for the G20*, Centre for Economic Policy Research.

Powers, W. and Riker, D. (2013), "Exchange rate pass-through in global value chains: The effects of upstream suppliers," No. 2013-02B, *Office of Economics Working Paper*, US International Trade Commission.

Prasad, E. (2009), "Is the Chinese growth miracle built to last?" *China Economic Review*, 20(1): 103–123.

Raj-Reichert, G. (2019), "Global value chains, contract manufacturers, and the middle-income trap: The electronics industry in Malaysia," *The Journal of Development Studies*, 56(4): 698–716.

Ren, Z. P. (2018), Seven reasons causing China–US trade imbalance, which cannot be solved by a trade war, *Sina Finance*, April, 1, 2018, https://finance.sina.com.cn/stock/marketresearch/2018-04-01/doc-ifysuxyz4050248.shtml.

Reuters (2020), UK PM Johnson orders for plans to end reliance on Chinese imports: The Times, *Reuters*, May 22, 2020.

Rodrik, D. (2006), "What's so special about China's exports?" *China & World Economy*, 14(5), 1–19.

Russell, C. (2019), "Adidas or Nike? Which retail giant is winning the sneakers war?" *Forbes*, August 22, 2019.

Salam, R. (2020), "Normalizing trade relations with China was a mistake," *The Atlantic*, June 8, 2018, https://www.theatlantic.com/ideas/archive/2018/06/normalizing-trade-relations-with-china-was-a-mistake/562403/.

Scott, R. E. (2015), *A Conservative Estimate of the Wal-Mart Effect*, Economic Policy Institute, December 9, 2015.

Sese, S. (2019), "Japan Inc. to speed up China exit in response to more tariffs," *Nikkei Asian Review*, August 5, 2019.

Sharma, K. and Gakuto, T. (2020), "Modi calls for 'trustworthy' supply chains, in alternative to China," *Nikkei Asian Review*, September 4, 2020.

Shimizu, K. (2020). "Huawei ban puts $26bn at risk for Japan, South Korea and Taiwan," *Nikkei Asian Review*, September 10, 2020.

Sim, D. (2020), "Singapore's Ho Ching thanks friends in Taiwan' after quibble over masks donation," *South China Morning Post*, April 13, 2020.

Sturgeon, T. J. and Kawakami, M. (2010), "Global value chains in the electronics industry: Was the crisis a window of opportunity for developing countries?" *Policy Research Working Paper*, No. 5417, The World Bank.

Sturgeon, T. J., Nielsen, P. B., Linden, G., Gereffi, G. and Brown, C. (2013), "Direct measurement of global value chains: Collecting product- and firm-level statistics on value added and business function outsourcing and offshoring," in A. Mattoo, Z. Wang and S. Wei (eds), *Trade in Value Added Developing New Measures of Cross-Border Trade*, The World Bank.

Sun, S. L., Chen H. and Pleggenkuhle-Miles, E. (2010), "Moving upward in global value chains: The innovations of mobile phone development in China," *Chinese Management Studies*, June 2010.

Tan, J. (2020), Anti-Huawei tech bans will hurt US more than China, *Nikkei Asian Review*, May 19, 2020.

Tanaka, A. (2019), Teardown of Huawei latest model shows reliance on US sourcing, *Nikkei Asian Review*, June 26, 2019,

Thelle, M. H. (2012), *Unchaining the Supply Chain: How Global Branded Clothing Firms are Contributing to the European Economy*, Copenhagen Economics, Copenhagen.

Thorbecke, W. (2006), "How would an appreciation of the Renminbi affect the US trade deficit with China?" *The BE Journal of Macroeconomics*, 8: 1–5.

Thorbecke, W. and Smith, G. (2010), "How would an appreciation of the Renminbi and the East Asian currencies affect China's exports?" *Review of International Economics*, 18(1): 95–108.

TrendForce (2018), "Apple Surpassed ASUS, Recording 9.6% Market Share in 2017 Global Notebook Market," https://www.trendforce.com/presscenter/news/20180212-9958.html.

UNCTAD (2013), *Global Value Chains and Development: Investment and Value Added Trade in the Global Economy*, UNCTAD, Geneva.

UNCTAD (2014), *Global Imports of Information Technology Goods Approach $2 Trillion*, www.uncatad.org (accessed on May 11, 2015).

UNIDO (2019), *Global Value Chains and Industrial Development: Lessons from China, South-East and South Asia.*

US Department of Commerce (2019), *Department of Commerce Announce the Addition of Huawei Technologies Co. Ltd to the Entity List*, May 15, 2019.

US Department of Commerce (2020), *Commerce Addresses Huawei's Efforts to Undermine Entity List, Restricts Products Designed and Produced with US Technologies*, May 15, 2020,

US Department of Treasury (2019), Treasury designates China as a currency manipulator, August 5, 2019.

Wakasugi, R. and Zhang, H. (2015), "Impacts of the World Trade Organization on Chinese exports," *RIETI Discussion Paper Series*, 15-E-021.

Wang, Y. (2006), "Cheap labor and China's export capacity," in K. H. Zhang (ed.), *China as the World Factory*, Routledge, 69–82.

Wang, Y. (2016), "OPPO explained: How a little-known smartphone company overtook Apple in China," *Forbes*, July 22, 2016.

Wang, Z. (1995), "The potential trade triangle among "Greater China," Japan and the United States," Paper presented at the Conference of "Challenges to the

World Trade Organization — Regionalism, labor and environmental standards," January 13, 1995, Hague, The Netherlands.

Whalley, J. and Xin, X. (2010), "China's FDI and non-FDI economies and sustainability of high Chinese growth," *China Economic Review*, 21(1): 123–135.

White House (2018), "President Donald J. Trump is confronting China's unfair trade policies," May 29, 2018.

Williams, A. (2020), "US lawmakers push to reclaim medical supply chains from China," *Financial Times*, April 2, 2020.

World Bank (2017), *Global Value Chain Development Report 2017: Measuring and Analyzing the Impact of GVCs on Economic Development*, Washington DC, World Bank.

World Bank (2018), World Development Indicators.

World Bank (2019), *Global Value Chain Development Report 2019: Technological Innovation, Supply Chain Trade and Workers in a Globalized World*, Washington, DC, World Bank.

WTO and IDE-JETRO (2011), *Trade Patterns and Global Value Chains in East Asia: From trade in Foods to Trade in Tasks*, WTO, Geneva.

Xing, Y. (2006a), "Why is China so attractive for FDI? The role of exchange rate," *China Economic Review*, 17(2): 198–209.

Xing, Y. (2006b), "Exchange rates and competition for FDI in Asia," *The World Economy*, 29(4): 419–434.

Xing, Y. (2012), "Processing trade, exchange rates and China's bilateral trade balances," *Journal of Asian Economics*, 23(5): 540–547.

Xing, Y. (2014), "China's high-tech exports: The myth and reality," *Asian Economic Papers*, 13(1): 109–123.

Xing, Y. (2018a), "Rising wages, yuan's appreciation and China's processing exports," *China Economic Review*, 48(c): 114–122.

Xing, Y. (2018b), "China–US trade war: A modern version of the Thucydides trap," *East Asian Policy*, 10(4): 5–23.

Xing, Y. (2020a), "How the iPhone widens the US trade deficit with China: The case of the iPhone X," *Frontiers of Economics in China*, 15(4): 642–658.

Xing, Y. (2020b), "Global value chains and the missing exports of the US," *China Economic Review*, 61(article 101429).

Xing, Y. and Detert, N. (2010), "How the iPhone widens the United States trade deficit with the PRC," *ADBI Working Paper 257*, Asian Development Bank Institute.

Xing, Y. and He, Y. (2018), "The Domestic Value added of Chinese Brand Mobile Phones," *Discussion Paper 18-09*, National Graduate Institute for Policy Studies, Tokyo.

Xinhua News (2019), "China ranked the No.1 recipient of FDI among developing countries for 27 years," October 30, 2019,

Yu, M. and Tian, W. (2019), "China's processing trade: A firm-level analysis," http://press-files.anu.edu.au/downloads/press/p182431/pdf/ch061.pdf.

Yu, Y. (2018), "A trade war that is unwarranted," *China & World Economy*, 26(5): 38–61.

Zebregs, H. and Tseng, W. S. (2002), "Foreign direct investment in China: Some lesson for other countries," *IMF Policy Discussion Paper No. 02/3*.

Zhang, K. H. and Song, S. (2000), "Promoting exports: The role of inward FDI in China," *China Economic Review*, 11: 285–396.

Index

Printed in the United States
by Baker & Taylor Publisher Services